SUPERBIKES OF THE SEVENTIES

Superbikes of the Seventies

by Roland Brown

Design by Tom Morgan

WORCESTERSHIRE COUNTY COUNCIL	
270	
Cypher	20.10.02
629.2275	£19.99

DAVID BULL PUBLISHING

CONTENTS

We recognize that some words, model names, and designations mentioned in this book are the property of the trademark holder. We use them only for identification purposes.

All photographs in this book were provided by the author, who owns their copyright. Photos by: Kevin Ash (Guzzi V7 Sport); Jack Burnicle (Benelli Sei, Bimota SB2, Ducati 900SS, Triumph T160, Yamaha XS1100); Jason Critchell (Morini); Patrick Gosling (Triumph X-75); Phil Masters (BMW R75/5, R90S, Honda CBX1000 action, MV Agusta 750 Sport, Suzuki GT750J); Mac McDiarmid (Laverda SFC); Oli Tennent (Guzzi S3, Le Mans action, Honda CB400F, GL1000, Kawasaki Mach IV, Z1-A action, Z1-R, Laverda Jota, MV Agusta Magni, Norton Commando S, Yamaha YR5). Other photos by the author, who also provided the brochures from his collection.

Library of Congress Control Number: 2002105026

ISBN 1-893618-17-X

David Bull Publishing, logo, and colophon are trademarks of David Bull Publishing, Inc.

Book and cover design: Tom Morgan, Blue Design, Portland, Maine (www.bluedes.com)

Printed in Hong Kong

10 9 8 7 6 5 4 3 2 1

David Bull Publishing
4250 East Camelback Road
Suite K150
Phoenix, AZ 85018
602-852-9500
602-852-9503 (fax)
www.bullpublishing.com

The motorcycles featured on the preceding pages are: page one, 1969 Honda CB750; page two, 1973 MV Agusta 750 Sport; page three, 1975 Laverda 750SF; page four, 1973 Moto Guzzi V7 Sport; page six, 1970 Norton Commando 750S. This page: 1975 Benelli 750 Sei.

9

AMF

Harley-Davidson
V-Twin Motorcycles

Acknowledgments

When José Codina and Ernest Ribé of Spanish bike magazine *Solo Moto* asked whether I'd be interested in testing some Sixties and Seventies bikes for a regular feature called "Motos de Leyenda" ("Legendary Bikes"), I didn't need any persuasion. The chance to ride around on some of the great old bikes that I am too young to have sampled first time around was simply too good to miss.

Back in 1993, I didn't realize that I'd still be digging out old bikes for "Motos de Leyenda" almost ten years later—or that I would eventually have the opportunity to bring some of them together into a book celebrating the first decade of the superbike. So I owe a big thanks to José and Ernest for asking me in the first place, as well as to David Bull for helping put some of the bikes together in one volume.

In this book's case, the need for thanks goes much farther than to the professionals—including photographers Kevin Ash, Jack Burnicle, Jason Critchell, Patrick Gosling, Phil Masters, Mac McDiarmid, and Oli Tennent—who have contributed to its production. *Superbikes of the Seventies* was possible only because of the generous help of all those people, from Bolton in Lancashire to Asheville in North Carolina, who lent me the bikes featured in these pages.

So it's a huge "Thanks, and safe riding" to all the following: Eamon Maloney (Honda CB750, Suzuki GT750, Yamaha XS750),

Trevor Gleadall of LP Williams Ltd (Triumph T150), Howard and Jed at Conquest Motorcycles (Norton Commando, Yamaha YR-5, BMW R75/5, Honda GL1000, Moto Guzzi 750 S3), Mick Phillips (Moto Guzzi V7 Sport), Kreton Hambos (Kawasaki H2 and Z1-R), Mike Lunsford (Triumph X-75), Paul Scanlon (Kawasaki Z1-A), Alan Clegg (Ducati 750 Sport), Alan Elderton (MV 750 Sport), David Lancaster (BMW R90S), Phil Clarke of Clarke's Classics (Ducati 860 GT), Andy Graveson (Benelli 750 Sei, Ducati 900SS, Bimota SB2), Brian Strickland (Triumph T160), Rick Proops of RAP Motorcycles (Honda CB400F), Steve Harris (Moto Guzzi Le Mans), Paul Shaw (Suzuki GT550), Stuart Mayhew of North Leicestershire Motorcycles (Moto Morinis), Steve Elliott and Richard Slater (Laverda SFC and Jota), Paul Riley (Harley XLCR), Pat Higgs of Higgs Motorcycles (Suzuki GS750), Mel Watkins (Honda CBX1000), Dave and Mark Kay of Eiger MV (Magni MV Agusta), Ron Scriven of Bikeworld (Suzuki GS1000), Chris Hadden (Yamaha XS1100), Ian Martin (Kawasaki Z1300), and Ray Sheepwash

(Laverda Mirage). Thanks also to the following for allowing use of extracts from magazine road tests: Mitch Boehm (*Motorcyclist*), Larry Little and David Edwards (*Cycle World*), Karla Sloggett (EMAP), and Grant Leonard (*SuperBike*).

Opposite: Harley's 1977 brochure shows the new XLCR Café Racer with the Sportster model from which it was developed. Sadly for H-D, halter tops and flares proved more popular style statements. Above: Suzuki hit the superbike battleground running, and haven't slowed up since. Right: Norton Triumph's 1975 Powerchoice was between Commando 850 twin and Trident 750 triple.

DUCATI 860

LAVERDA 750 SF

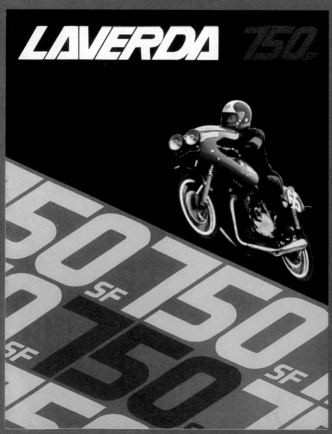

12

Introduction

Motorcycling came of age in the Seventies—the decade of the superbike. That short period saw an explosion of excitement, technology, and performance. In just ten years the two-wheeled world was transformed, from a monochrome scene of traditional single- and twin-cylinder machines—as served up by European and American manufacturers for several decades—to a colorful riot of twins, triples, fours, and sixes of all shapes, sizes, and origins.

Japan led the way, of course. Most notably Honda, whose CB750 took motorcycle design to new levels and set the standard for all that followed. In motorcycling terms, the Seventies really started in 1969 with the glamorous four's introduction. The modern era had arrived—and from then on, things just got better and better. Motorcyclists demanded more performance, more variety, more technology—and they were not disappointed.

Honda's Japanese rivals countered with superbikes of their own, in contrasting styles—Kawasaki's banzai two-stroke triples and potent fours and Suzuki's softer two-strokes and, later, sophisticated four-strokes. By the end of the decade, two-stroke specialist Yamaha had also joined the battle with distinctive three- and four-cylinder machines. For the wide-eyed buyer, it was a dazzling array from which to choose.

And it was by no means just the Japanese who made the Seventies such a golden age for motorcycling. To the contrary, many of the best bikes were from elsewhere: Ducati and Moto Guzzi V-twins, plus fiery Laverdas and smooth-running Benellis from Italy; boxers of increasing sophistication from BMW; and triples as well as twins from Triumph. Even Harley joined in with a V-twin superbike of its own.

The development of two-wheeled performance through the decade can be clearly traced through the pages of this book, which is set out with the bikes listed in chronological order of their arrival on the market. Deciding which to include was difficult. The term "superbike" is a subjective one that here was deemed to refer to a roadgoing machine of outstanding performance—either in a straight line or, in the case of some smaller, sporty bikes, on a twisty road.

The Seventies saw huge advances in engine technology, while chassis design remained based on traditional steel-tube, twin-shock layouts that had been adequate for 50 BHP twins, but were in many cases stretched by multis of twice that output. The decade also saw the emergence of frame specialists such as Bimota and Magni. Only in the Eighties would the chassis design of mass-produced superbikes truly catch up with their engine performance.

Horsepower-related handling problems were one symptom of an industry that was only just under control as motorcycling roared and sometimes wobbled and weaved through the Seventies, heading for that ultimate icon of excess, Kawasaki's gigantic six-cylinder Z1300. In many ways it was a crazy ride—and it sure was an exciting one, too.

Opposite: This seductive combination of Ducati and girl earned a prominent position on many teenagers' bedroom walls, including the author's. Laverda's 750cc twin and Kawasaki 903cc Z1 four offered contrasting routes to high performance. Above: Honda's CBX1000 tank decal emphasized the big Six's sporting intent.

Honda CB750

I had expected this immaculate CB750 to be good, but I had never imagined that it would be so... well, *exciting*. As I followed a line of cars at about 50 mph (80 km/h), a gap appeared in the oncoming traffic, and I trod down a gear and wound open the throttle to overtake. The Honda responded instantly—not just with a burst of acceleration that was impressive for a bike that was built several decades ago, but with a throaty four-pipe roar that made me want to take it right to the red-line.

Suddenly I'm back in 1970 or thereabouts, devouring everything on the road aboard the greatest production motorcycle the world has ever seen. Head down, hold those high bars tight, let's make that motor really sing! I've got breathtaking acceleration and 120 mph-plus (195 km/h-plus) top speed on tap, with levels of reliability and sophistication that until now have never been approached. In short, I'm riding the world's first true superbike—and it feels mighty good.

If a brief blast of CB750 acceleration is enough to get the adrenalin flowing all these years later, what must it have felt like to those lucky enough to ride Honda's hotshot when it was new?

Compared to the relatively crude pushrod twins that were the best that most motorcyclists had experienced, the CB750 was a machine from a different world. With its unprecedented combination of powerful and smooth four-cylinder engine, five-speed gearbox, electric starter, and front disc brake, the Honda redefined motorcyclists' perception of speed and technology overnight.

A mouth-watering specification and competitive price were part of the appeal, but the CB750's main attraction was simply its uniquely seductive quartet of cylinders and pipes. Honda's racing heritage was obvious in its layout, although the roadster differed from the predominantly 16-valve, DOHC racers in using a single camshaft, driven by a chain up the center of the engine, and only

Opposite: Honda's 736cc four had a single overhead camshaft and an electric starter, produced 67 BHP and was superbly reliable. Top: The CB750 wasn't just the "first superbike," it was arguably the most significant motorcycle of all time. Right: High bars meant the rider caught the wind at speed, but at least the motor was smooth.

two valves per cylinder. Despite this, the CB750's 67 BHP output gave it the edge over even the most exotic European machines.

The capacity of 736cc was achieved by long-stroke dimensions of 61 x 63 mm, which helped reduce engine width. Another feature unusual for Honda was the dry sump, which was also chosen to save bulk. Designed as an all-rounder with particular emphasis on the American market, the Honda was a physically big machine with a broad seat and high, wide handlebars.

This bike had covered 29,000 miles (47,000 km) in total, but very few since being restored to good-as-new condition. Virtually its only flaw was a tired battery that made starting on the button a less reliable affair than in its prime. No problem, because early 750s were fitted with a kick-start for such emergencies. The motor burst into life with a potent-sounding blend of engine whirring and exhaust note that would be far too loud for modern legislation, and added considerably to the thrill of the ride.

The Honda was just about as fast as any bike on the road when it was launched, backing up its top speed with a standing quarter time of under 13 seconds, plus a reasonable spread of low and midrange power. Even now its clutch felt light, its gearbox slick, its whole powerplant efficient and strong. (Contemporary road tests told of prototype motors being run at 6000 RPM for 200 hours and at the 8500 RPM red-line for 20 hours during development, something that simply did not happen in most European factories.)

Of course, the Honda's level of performance barely matches that of a modern bike of half the capacity. Even in its day the bike had clearly been designed for flexibility, ease of use, and reasonable fuel consumption, as well as for sheer speed. But I was still pleasantly surprised by just how lively it felt. It pulled crisply through the midrange and surged forward again at higher revs, with the benefit of that atmospheric four-pipe howl that added to the impression of speed.

Like so many Honda fours since, it cruised effortlessly and

Honda CB750 (1969)

Engine type	Air-cooled SOHC, 8-valve transverse four
Displacement	736cc
Bore x stroke	61 x 63 mm
Compression ratio	9:1
Carburetion	4 x 28 mm Keihins
Claimed power	67 BHP @ 8000 RPM
Transmission	5-speed
Electrics	12 V battery, 210 W generator
Frame	Tubular steel duplex cradle
Front suspension	Telescopic, no adjustment
Rear suspension	Twin shock absorbers, adjustable preload
Front brake	Single 290 mm (11.5 in) disc
Rear brake	178 mm (7 in) SLS drum
Front tire	3.25 x 19 in
Rear tire	4.00 x 18 in
Wheelbase	1450 mm (57 in)
Seat height	800 mm (31.5 in)
Fuel capacity	17 liters (3.7 UK gal, 4.5 US gal)
Weight	230 kg (506 lb) wet

Right: Unlike most modern fours, the CB750 engine used dry-sump lubrication, so it had an oil tank below the seat on the right side. Note the kick-starter to back up the electric start. Below right: The big single front disc brake gave notably more bite and reliability than drums of most other bikes. It was also an important sales feature that would soon become commonplace among manufacturers. Protective fork gaiters were a practical touch.

smoothly at the legal limit with plenty of acceleration in hand, yet was also totally docile around town. Controls and switches were light and easy, though the clutch was slightly grabby, so much so that a couple of times I stalled when pulling away from the lights.

Perhaps inevitably, the CB750's chassis was no match for its engine, but by the standards of the day the Honda's handling was not at all bad. Although quite heavy, the four carried its weight well, thanks partly to firm suspension that gave a rather harsh ride over bumps and potholes. Very aggressive riding, especially on a track, could make a CB750 lose its cool—as UK mag *Motor Cycle Mechanics*' tester "discovered at around 80 mph [130 km/h] on a bumpy bend, when the front end seemed light and gave one or two heart-stopping twitches as the power was poured on through the bend."

Right: All a CB750 rider had to do to see over 120mph (195km/h) on the speedometer was find a straight piece of road, wind back the throttle, and hold on tight. The rev-counter was red-lined at 8500rpm, and peak power arrived just 500rpm earlier, but the Honda was very flexible and didn't need revving hard to go fast.

This bike gave no such drama, though admittedly I wasn't riding as hard as I would a new machine. Steering required a fair amount of effort, although the wide bars helped counter the heavy feel given by its conservative geometry and 19-inch front wheel. Ground clearance was rated excellent three decades ago, and there was quite enough for the grip provided by a pair of original Bridgestone tires.

I was surprised to find myself impressed by the four's single front disc brake, which gave plenty of stopping power provided the lever was squeezed hard. The big 290 mm (11.5 in) disc was regarded as one of the Honda's key attractions when the bike was launched, and it would lead the move away from drum brakes on high-performance machines. It's a shame the single-leading-shoe rear drum was contrastingly grabby.

In most respects, Honda was rather slow to improve the CB750 through the Seventies, and by no means all the changes that were made were beneficial. As the decade progressed, the 750 began to fall victim to the steady detuning process necessary to reduce emissions and satisfy American environmentalists. Later CB750

K-series models were slower than the original 1969 model (known as the K0 in the States), let alone Kawasaki's 900cc Z1 and its derivatives.

Even the sportier F1 and F2 models produced later in the decade couldn't live up to the first four's musclebike image. But if the CB750's reign as world's greatest superbike was short, its influence would be felt for a very long time. This bike gave motorcycling a new dimension. It broadened riders' horizons beyond the traditional parallel twin, and single-handedly shifted the balance of power from England to Japan.

When you ride an example as nice as this, compare its performance and specification with those of its leading contemporaries—those relatively simple, suddenly old-fashioned European twins and Harleys—and consider the way its four-cylinder sophistication has shaped more recent machines, the CB750's status as motorcycling's all-time great is hard to deny.

From *Cycle World*, AUG. 1969

"Tired of people not noticing? In past years, motorcycling marked you as a man apart... You glowed inside, glad that you had something that the common man didn't share. But now everyone rides a motorcycle, and you've stopped waving to the other guy, and things don't seem the same any more.

The only thing that could relight your fire is the very best road bike in the world. It would have to be extravagant, so that the envious bystander would be forced to say, "But who really needs all that," proudly thumping the tank of his leaky Twin. It would also have to be extremely functional. Roadable. Comfortable. Responsive.

Owning a bike like this, you could thumb your nose at the Honda Motor Company, which is most responsible for seeing that hordes of new riders crowd you on your private road. But if you had the finest of all production machines, this two-wheeled answer to Ferrari-Porsche-Lamborghini, you would be riding a Honda 750cc four-cylinder. Soichiro-San would have the last laugh."

Norton
Commando 750S

My ride on the bright yellow Commando had not started well. The big twin-cylinder engine had required several leaps on the kickstarter before finally bursting into life. The front drum brake's new shoes had needed bedding-in before working properly, and when I'd finally reached the open road and wound open the throttle, the clutch had started slipping as soon as the engine began to work hard.

But what a difference a few hours' riding made! Starting my final ride, the Norton motor fired-up first time in response to my practiced leap on the lever, emitting a deep bellow through the side-by-side pipes. As I reluctantly rode back to return the bike to its owner, the front brake was working much better and the clutch was fine, even when the motor's mighty midrange acceleration was used to the full.

Falling in love with a motorbike is dangerously easy when it's as pretty and distinctive as this yellow Norton. Few bikes are more interesting from the left side than the right, but the Commando S, which was built for only a short time in 1969 and 1970, is one

Left: Norton's Isolastic system, whose rubber engine mount is visible at the front of the crankcase, prevented most of the Commando's parallel twin vibration from reaching the rider. Above: High bars, yellow paint, and lots of chrome make a handsome bike. Right: Handling was to Norton's traditional high standard.

Frontrunning!

For the fourth record-breaking year Norton Commando again

VOTED MACHINE OF THE YEAR

By the readers of Motorcycle News

NOW A QUADRUPLE WINNER

of them. Those twin high-level pipes, beautifully set off by perforated heat shields, combine with the high handlebars and compact tank and engine unit to give a timeless appeal.

Norton had introduced the Commando, with conventional lower pipes on each side, back in April 1968. The Birmingham firm's parallel twin lineage stretched back to the 500cc Dominator of 1949, and the new model was a big hit from the word go. Its angled-forward 746cc engine, based on the same-size Atlas unit, thundered out an increased output of 58 BHP at 6400 RPM, and incorporated mods including higher compression, a bigger alternator, triplex instead of single-row primary chain, plus a car-style clutch with four plates and a single diaphragm spring.

It was partly to satisfy the American export market, where Atlas-based desert bikes were popular and many machines were offered with high-level pipes, that Norton introduced the Commando 750S in March 1969. In addtion to its high bars and pipes, the S also had a smaller fiberglass gas tank, which it shared with the year's other new model, the more conventional Commando R. Both models had a revised Mk II engine with new ignition points and revised rev-counter drive. Slightly increased compression ratio of 9:1, combined with the free-breathing reverse-cone pipes, increased peak output to 60 BHP.

Norton retained the ingenious Isolastic system that had already become an important part of the Commando's appeal. The frame's main large-diameter steel spine held a cradle of smaller-diameter tubes that supported the engine/gearbox unit, the shakings of which were isolated from the rider by the Isolastic system's trio of rubber mounts. Other changes included exposed (instead of gaitered) forks and a conventional seat instead of the original Fastback item. Extra chrome on details, including mudguard stays and gearlever, added to the flamboyant image.

The front runners

first the sprinter…

and now a long distance strider

Right: The Commando S, with its high handlebars and exhaust system, was created for the US market, especially the West Coast where desert racing was popular. The S had style but was not a great success, even in California. Although the model was short-lived, it was replaced by the similarly styled Street Scrambler. Below: Instruments and headlamp had plenty of chrome.

At some stage this bike's motor had been replaced by the bored-out, 829cc motor that Norton introduced to power the 850 Commando in 1973. Purists would doubtless be horrified by this and several other later-model parts, including the front fender and speedometer. But this Commando lost nothing in my eyes by having the softer, torquier, and generally more oil-tight 850 motor, for which Norton initially claimed an identical 60 BHP peak output.

In typical Commando fashion, this bike needed a fierce lunge at the kick-start to turn it over. But if started correctly, it always fired-up in a couple of kicks. Once the clutch-slip—a typical result of its recent inactivity—had cleared, the motor was wonderful, pulling from very low revs with an eager throttle response

Norton Commando 750S (1970)

Engine type	Air-cooled pushrod, 2-valve parallel twin
Displacement	745cc (829cc)
Bore x stroke	73 x 89 mm (this bike 77 x 89 mm)
Compression ratio	9:1
Carburetion	2 x 30 mm Amal Concentric (32 mm)
Claimed power	60 BHP @ 6400 RPM
Transmission	4-speed gearbox
Electrics	12 V battery
Frame	Steel spine; twin downtube with Isolastic rubber mounts
Front suspension	Norton Roadholder telescopic
Rear suspension	Twin shock absorbers with 5-way preload adjustment
Front brake	203 mm (8 in) TLS drum
Rear brake	178 mm (7 in) SLS drum
Front tire	3.25 x 19 in
Rear tire	4.00 x 19 in
Wheelbase	1441 mm (56 in)
Fuel capacity	10 liters (2.25 UK gal, 2.7 US gal)
Weight	185 kg (407 lb) dry

Below: The Commando S was powered by Norton's Mk II engine, with revised ignition points, increased compression ratio, and reverse-cone pipes. This modified machine has a later 829cc engine, with extra midrange and unchanged 60 BHP peak output.

made more thrilling by the hung-out-to-dry riding position and guttural exhaust growl.

There was too much traffic around to get close to the Norton's likely top speed of about 115 mph (185 km/h), but it surged toward the ton mark enthusiastically. More to the point, the Commando was happy to cruise at an indicated 80 mph (130 km/h) for as long as I cared to hold on to those high bars. Its four-speed gearchange was impressively precise, too. There was a little bit of vibration through seat and footrests, despite the Isolastics. But the Commando was smooth enough to make me realize how much of an edge the system must have given over rival parallel twins, if not over Honda's recently released CB750-four.

Its chassis was also good enough to maintain Norton's reputation for fine handling. Despite the high bars, the Commando was stable at speed. And although its steering wasn't exactly quick, due to old-style geometry and 19-inch wheels, the 185 kg (407 lb) bike felt reasonably light and flickable. Suspension was fairly firm, especially at the rear, which helped handling but gave a slightly harsh ride over bigger bumps.

Back in 1970 the 750S was less popular than its conventional siblings, and it was soon dropped (although a similarly styled, and even shorter-lived, 750SS model was produced in the following year). With its high bars and tiny tank, this was far from the most practical Norton ever made. But if it's style, torque, handling, and charisma you're after, the Commando 750S has got the lot.

From *Motorcyclist*, Aug. 1969

"Now comes the second generation Commando, the S model aimed straight at the sporting rider who wants top performance allied to good looks and does not mind paying for it.

It had that Norton feel—taut and responsive, with real power coming from low, low down the rev range. This wide spread of power made the Commando S easy to ride. You could trickle along at near walking pace, crack open the throttle and away you'd go with the exhaust note rising to a pleasant crescendo behind you.

Top speed is well into the 120 zone, with 100 mph coming up in a rush in third. Of course, the joy of it all is that it is done without vibration, the curse of so many otherwise good bikes. Yes, the Commando S is the best Norton yet, and one which will win many new friends for the famous name which goes right back to 1907, when a Norton won the twin cylinder class of the very first Isle of Man TT."

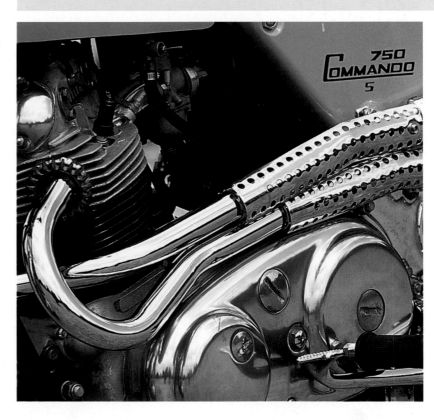

Yamaha YR5

Memories can be so misleading. As I turned on the 350cc twin's ignition and unfolded the kickstart for the first time, my head was already spinning with thoughts of good times aboard previous Yamaha two-strokes. The acceleration of my old race-tuned RD400C; the brilliant 350LC that I once thrashed across Europe; the spine-tingling scream of a 350 Power Valve with its throttle wound back to the stop.

This time wasn't quite like that. The motor crackled into life easily, and a few minutes later I was cruising contentedly along at about 60 mph (97 km/h). But when I came to a straight and cracked open the throttle, the Yamaha's acceleration was gentle rather than dramatic. And when I reached the first good bend, my expectations of nimble handling were shattered by the reality of this bike's grabby front brake, diving forks, and rather vague steering.

That's what happens when you mix memories of bikes spanning over a decade. Or, even worse, when you fall into the trap of judging a classic machine by modern standards. This Yam was in good

nick with just 12,000 miles (19,300 km) on its clock—but it was, after all, a twin-cylinder bike built as long ago as 1970, and with a peak power output of just 36 BHP at 7000 RPM. Expecting it to provide blood-curdling acceleration all these years later was just a little unfair.

The YR5—known simply as the R5 in the States—was a real star in its day, though. Yamaha came late to four-stroke super-bikes, releasing its debut model, the XS750, only in 1977. But the firm's dynasty of two-stroke middleweights provided some of the great bikes of the Seventies and Eighties, with a near-unbeatable blend of performance and value. And while the RD400 and the later, liquid-cooled LCs are more familiar to most riders, the models that started the legend were the air-cooled RD350 and the YR5, its look-alike predecessor.

Opposite: The Yamaha's light weight helped give it good handling when new, but its suspension did not improve with age. Above: Lean roadster styling was retained for the long-running RD350 model that followed. Right: Acceleration was lively, but riders hoping to see 100mph (161km/h) on the speedo were disappointed.

Right: The largest of Yamaha's family of two-stroke twins was a 347cc unit with piston-ported induction, five-speed gearbox, and peak output of 36BHP. The firm's racetrack development resulted in rapid improvements, notably the introduction of reed valves and a six-speed box to create the RD350 in 1973. Below right: The YR5's twin-downtube frame was reasonably stiff, but its slender front forks had soft springs and lacked damping.

In 1970, the year the this model was launched, Rod Gould won Yamaha's fourth 250cc world championship, following fellow Brit Phil Read's three titles in the Sixties. Its design could be traced back to the YR1 of 1967, and was shaped both by racetrack development and by Yamaha's smaller roadsters. The YR5 was the biggest of a visually near-identical family of 250, 200, and 125cc twins. Like the smaller models, the YR5 used a piston-ported, 180-degree crankshaft motor, in this case with dimensions of 64 x 54 mm for a capacity of 347cc.

Yamaha claimed that the YR5's steel, twin-downtube frame was designed using knowledge gained through racing, where privateer Yams were already becoming popular. Suspension was the typical combination of narrow forks and preload-adjustable rear shocks, holding 18-inch diameter wire-spoked wheels. Brakes were drums at both ends, with a twin-leading-shoe unit up front.

Yamaha YR5 (1971)

Engine type	Air-cooled parallel twin two-stroke
Displacement	347cc
Bore x stroke	64 x 54 mm
Compression ratio	6.9:1
Carburetion	2 x 28 mm Mikunis
Claimed power	36 BHP @ 7000 RPM
Transmission	5-speed
Electrics	12 V battery; 35/35 W headlamp
Frame	Tubular steel duplex cradle
Front suspension	Telescopic, no adjustment
Rear suspension	Twin shock absorbers, adjustable preload
Front brake	183 mm (7.2 in) TLS drum
Rear brake	183 mm (7.2 in) SLS drum
Front tire	3.00 x 18 in
Rear tire	3.50 x 18 in
Wheelbase	1341 mm (53 in)
Seat height	790 mm (31 in)
Fuel capacity	12 liters (2.6 UK gal, 3.2 US gal)
Weight	150 kg (330 lb) wet

Skinny and simply built, the YR5 weighed just 150 kg (330 lb) with half a tank of fuel, and at a standstill it felt light and maneuverable. Its mixture of burbling, rattling tickover noise and the unmistakable smell of two-stroke oil brought back memories of other Yamahas. For what was in its day a hard-and-fast sportster, the handlebars seemed ridiculously high. Forward-set footrests and the thick dual-seat added to the almost relaxed feel.

So did the YR5's straight-line performance, for the little twin didn't come close to providing the high-revving thrills that I had expected. Why I had, I'm not quite sure. Some modern 125cc sportbikes make almost as much power, after all. Flat-out on an open road, the less-than-aerodynamic YR5 ran out of steam before 100 mph (160 km/h) however hard I tried to hide behind the clocks.

At least the Yam had a broad spread of power, pulling cleanly and fairly smoothly from below 3000 RPM to the red-line. That enabled it to cruise at an indicated 90 mph (145 km/h), though

From *Cycle World*, JUN. 1970

"Winding roads, downtown traffic or 70 mph freeway grind, nothing seemed to make much difference to this stout two-stroke. Power is on tap from well down in the rev range to around 8000 RPM, where it begins to taper off. Mid range torque is noticeably better than with previous models, as the R5 pulls like a 500 when you twist the grip in fifth.

The R5 may be described as a quick handling machine. As it has most of its weight down low, there is little top hamper to inhibit the rider from pitching the machine aggressively through his favorite set of bends... We would like to see the wheelbase extended slightly to slow down the quick handling and put more weight on the front wheel.

The R5 offers substance, as well as appearance. Within limits, it will do things most of the more expensive superbikes will do, at lesser cost but equal fun value."

hills would knock that figure down to 85 mph. High speeds soon became tiring, of course, thanks to wind blast from the upright riding position. Comfort was much better at slower speeds, though the YR5 didn't like being treated too gently. American riders who stuck to the freeway speed limit found spark plugs prone to fouling.

Contemporary tests described the YR5 as a quick-handling machine, with its weight down low, good suspension, and excellent traction from its tires. This YR5's handling was certainly fairly quick. Despite the bike's 18-inch front wheel and old-fashioned steering geometry, the combination of light weight, wide handlebars, and narrow front tire meant it could be flicked into bends rapidly and effortlessly.

Underdamped suspension at both ends ensured that it wasn't a good idea to get too aggressive, though. The soft forks and the Yam's rear-end weight bias made the YR5 feel very twitchy at the front, while even fairly modest cornering speeds had the rear end wallowing, too. Doubtless this bike's shocks had deteriorated with age, but even so it was obvious why so many riders fitted aftermarket units.

This bike's front drum brake had plenty of power but was rather fierce, especially considering the narrow, ribbed front tire

through which its power was being transmitted. Despite the tires, it wasn't hard to get the footpegs touching down.

In case all that sounds too critical, I should add that riding the YR5 was still great fun, at least on a twisty road, provided allowances were made for its age. And that's how it should be—because make no mistake, this was the poor boy's superbike of its time. Back in 1971, when this particular machine was built, it would have taken a well-ridden example of Honda's CB750 to stay ahead of the screaming stroker on anything but a long straight road.

The same could be said of this bike's two-stroke successors such as the RD350, RD400, and RD350LC, as they continued to give larger bikes a difficult time for many more years. They were fast, furious, light, agile, good-looking, and unbeatable value for money. Just like the original YR5 itself.

Above left: For such a small bike the YR5 was rapid in a straight line, and rewarded spirited riding with giant-killing performance. This model and other Yamaha two-strokes perhaps did more than any others to bring a racetrack spirit to the street. Decades later the Yam's performance seemed slightly tame, but its revvy nature and high-pitched exhaust note added plenty of excitement.

Kawasaki 750 Mach IV

Nobody could say they weren't warned about Kawasaki's 750cc triple. At a glance, the two-stroke looks harmless enough. It's nicely styled and simply built, its engine compact despite large cooling fins. Then you notice that in addition to the friction-type steering damper at the headstock, there is a second, hydraulic damper—an official factory option, mounted on a special lug welded to the frame. Even Kawasaki's engineers knew this bike was seriously crazy.

Of all the early-Seventies superbikes, the Kawasaki that was known as the H2 or Mach IV had the most evil reputation. Outrageous speed, explosive power delivery, and marginal handling were combined with excessive noise, smoke, and thirst to produce the ultimate bad-boy's motorbike. It's doubtful whether any other two-wheeler was quite as antisocial as this. Or whether any other firm than Kawasaki, fast becoming *the* marque for high performance when the H2 appeared in 1972—hot on the heels of the similar 500cc H1 triple—would have built it.

The format was simple, and centered on the 748cc three-pot motor that was basically an enlarged and strengthened version of the H1/Mach III unit. The extra capacity, along with milder exhaust porting and ignition timing, allowed a slightly wider spread of torque than that of the notoriously peaky H1 (itself a fearsome machine). More importantly, the bigger bike's power output was increased to a maximum of 74 BHP at 6800 RPM, considerably more than rivals such as Honda's 750-four and Suzuki's GT750.

Much of the rest of the Mach IV was similar to the smaller triple, too, including the conventional twin-downtube steel frame. The forks held wire wheels, in 19-inch front and 18-inch rear diameters, with twin shocks and a brake combination of a single front disc and rear drum. Gentle, rounded styling and high handlebars added

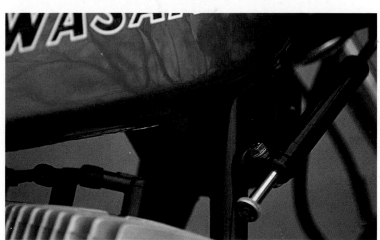

Opposite: High handlebars combined with fearsome acceleration to make the Mach IV the perfect bike for wheelies. Above: The 750's profile was almost identical to that of the 500cc Mach III, which had been terrorizing the streets for several years. Right: Hydraulic steering damper hinted at the triple's reputation for evil handling.

Kawasaki **72** ⭐⭐⭐ **K**

year of the **tri-stars**

to the Kawasaki's deceptively normal, almost laid-back, appearance.

There was certainly nothing remotely ordinary about the Mach IV's straight-line performance, which made the Kawa a match for any bike on the road back in '72. Top speed was a highly competitive 120 mph (193 km/h). And the two-stroke's relatively light weight (210 kg/462 lb) meant it got there very quickly, rocketing through the standing quarter-mile in 12.5 seconds.

Kawasaki didn't hold back when it came to establishing the triple's performance credentials. One brochure proclaimed that: "The Kawasaki 750 Mach IV has only one purpose in life: to give you the most exciting and exhilarating performance. It's so quick it demands the razor-sharp reactions of an experienced rider. It's a machine you must take seriously."

Soon the press echoed those words, describing the triple as "the ultimate machismo street cycle" and "the nastiest, meanest motorcycle ever to wrench the wrist muscles of the know-it-all biker." Tales of the Mach IV's outrageous behavior spread fast, and centered not just on the bike's sheer speed but also on its handling. Words such as "wheelie" and "tankslapper" started cropping up in road tests.

All of which was enough to make me approach the H2 with plenty of respect. Simply firing up this immaculate 1972-model triple was an experience. Ignition on, lift up the right footpeg, hold down the choke lever with my right thumb and *kick*. The motor burst into life with a deafening mixture of mechanical rattle and crackle from the three exhaust pipes, which belched blue smoke while I blipped the throttle.

Neutral is at the bottom of the gearbox so I hooked up into gear with my left boot, let out the rather stiff clutch, and pulled away. For a bike with such a reputation for speed and violence, the

Mach IV initially felt surprisingly docile. The trio of 32 mm Mikuni carbs gave a reasonably crisp response from 3000 RPM or lower, and the Kawa could happily be cruised along without need for repeated glances at the tach.

But it wasn't until I dropped it down a couple of cogs and opened it up that the Mach IV came alive. At about 5000 RPM the exhaust note turned into a shriek, and the bike leapt forward in a frenzied charge, tach needle waving madly across the dial in the vicinity of the 7500 RPM red-line. Moments later the triple was ripping through the 100 mph (160 km/h) mark—rider hanging on tight and grinning broadly—with plenty more to come.

Sheer speed was the H2's main claim to fame, but the triple is also remembered for its marginal handling. Many of the horror stories were exaggerated, but anyone planning to make use of the bike's performance was well advised to fit the factory's hydraulic damper—and even that couldn't always prevent a hard-ridden H2's handlebars from flapping disturbingly at times.

This bike was reassuringly stable, perhaps helped by the modern Conti that replaced the original ribbed front tire. But hitting one particular bump with the bike well cranked over sent a warning through the bars that the triple was not to be pushed too far. Anyone foolish enough to have allowed the powerband to bite in the middle of a bend would have left an H2-sized hole in the hedge some distance down the road.

Riders who did get into trouble could at least rely on a front disc brake that was better than most of the drums with which

Kawasaki 750 Mach IV H2 (1972)

Engine type	Air-cooled two-stroke triple
Displacement	748cc
Bore x stroke	71 x 63 mm
Compression ratio	7:1
Carburetion	3 x 32 mm Mikunis
Claimed power	74hp @ 6800 RPM
Transmission	5-speed
Electrics	12 V battery
Frame	Tubular steel duplex cradle
Front suspension	Telescopic, no adjustment
Rear suspension	Twin shock absorbers, adjustable preload
Front brake	Single 295 mm (11.6 in) disc; second disc optional extra
Rear brake	203 mm (8 in) SLS drum
Front tire	3.25 x 19 in
Rear tire	4.00 x 18 in
Wheelbase	1410 mm (55.5 in)
Seat height	800 mm (31.5 in)
Fuel capacity	18 liters (4 UK gal, 4.7 US gal)
Weight	210 kg wet (462 lb)

Below: Kawasaki was not exaggerating when billing the Mach IV as motorcycling's most powerful 750. Honda's CB750 and Suzuki's GT750 were 7 BHP down on official outputs. More potent still was the 100 BHP-plus H2R racing derivative, an unreliable, ill-handling beast ridden by factory stars including Paul Smart, Yvon Duhamel, and Art Bauman.

From *Bike*, Nov. 1974

"This bike is capable of hauling ass very fast indeed: about 100 miles per hour in 13 seconds capable, in fact. Such acceleration will satisfy even the most mind-wrenched adrenalin addict.

It also handles in a manner strange to those bred on British or Italian vehicles, which is not undesirable once mastered. As I think you may understand by now, the performance potential of this bike is so vastly superior to most other two wheeled products that if poke is your main criterion, such things as riding position, economy and durability are things you'll learn to live with or adapt to your secondary requirements."

rival bikes were fitted back in '72. Even so, after a series of hard stops had reduced the brake's initial bite, I could appreciate why many H2 pilots invested in the optional second disc and caliper.

One aspect of the triple's performance that nobody could do much about was its thirst. Many riders averaged less than 25 mpg, and figures of below 20 mpg were common. But plenty of riders were prepared to put up with poor economy for performance, and the Mach IV was a hit, especially in the States. Kawasaki kept building it for several years, introducing numerous modifications through A, B, and C models while retaining the bike's basic look and feel.

The 1974-model H2-B's engine was revised to reduce emissions, but there was little that Kawasaki could do about the triple's antisocial nature. Increasing environmental awareness meant that the fiery two-stroke's days were numbered. A few years later the H2 had disappeared—leaving behind it a trail of blue smoke and a reputation that time has done little to diminish.

The most powerful 750 superbike

750 MACH IV model H2

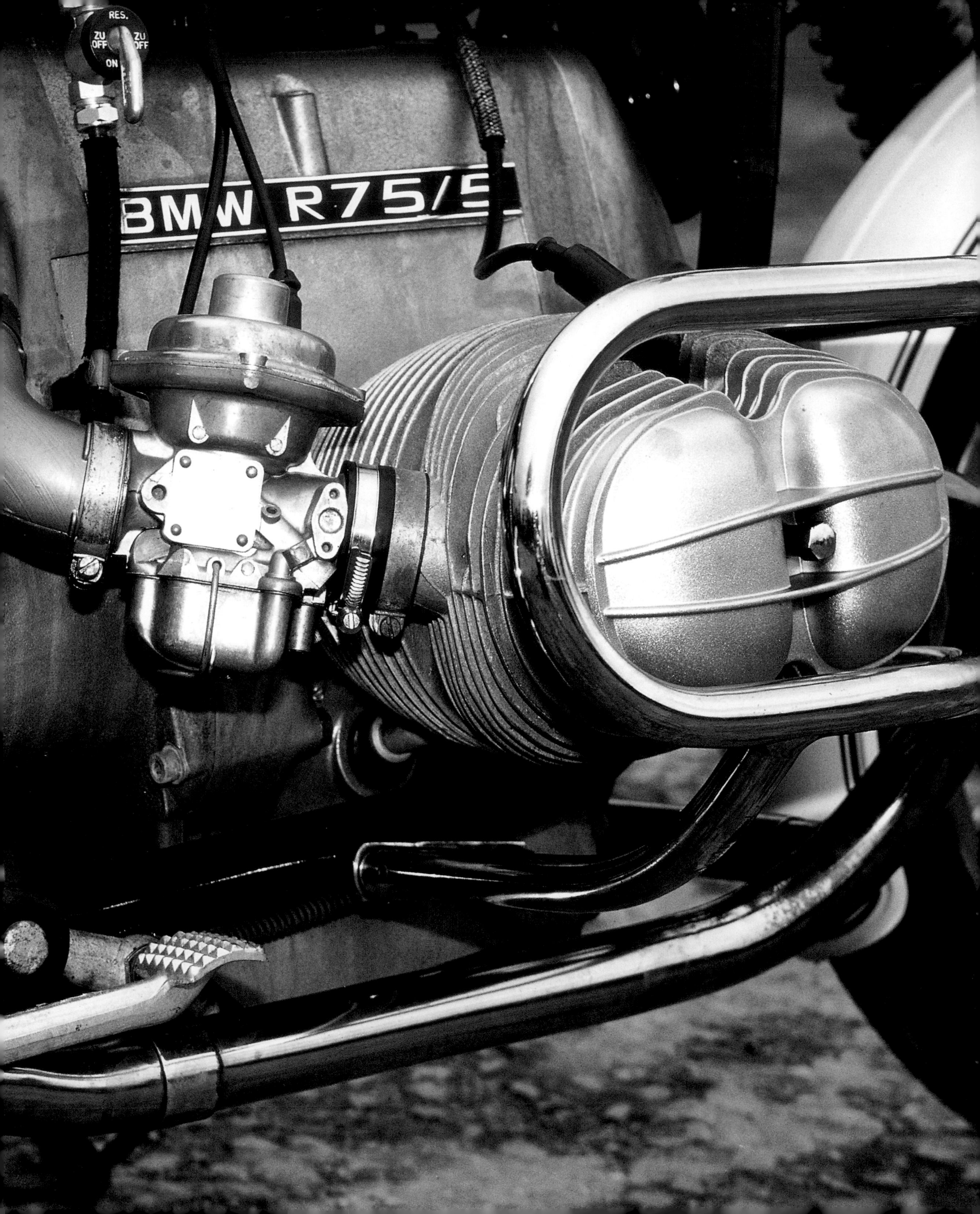
RES.
ZU
OFF
ZU
OFF
ON
BMW R75/5

BMW R75/5

It was one of those dark, blustery winter days, when the weather makes its presence felt with every trip on a motorbike. A cold, strong wind was shaking the trees. The roads were still damp in places from overnight rain; the sky looked threatening although the forecasted rain had yet to arrive.

Through it all the R75/5 purred on serenely: smooth, comfortable, stable. Effortlessly and rapidly putting the road under its wheels, it turned what could have been an unpleasant trip into a very enjoyable ride. Despite the conditions, I felt myself wishing I was not just taking the aging boxer for a short spin, but setting off for some far-flung destination, where its touring prowess could really be put to the test.

This R75/5 had doubtless inspired many similarly ambitious thoughts when it was new back in 1972, three years after the model had been introduced along with the R60/5 and R50/5. Although the three boxers clearly still owed much to Max Fritz's original R32 of 1923, they marked the start of a new era for BMW. Their design was more modern, emphasized by their

telescopic forks in place of the previous Earles design. And the bikes were assembled on a new line at Spandau in Berlin, leaving the previous Munich factory to the expanding car division.

The 75/5's chassis was not quite new, having previously been used by BMW's International Six Days Trials machines. It's also true that telescopic forks had been available to special order on the American-market R69US, R60US, and R50US roadsters since 1967. But for BMW it was still a bold move to drop the distinctive cradle frame and Earles forks for which the

What a motorcycle is worth, cannot be established only from the horse-power. Or from the maximum speed stated in the catalogue. But from the power brought on

Left: BMW's trademark flat-twin engine layout dated back to the 500cc R32 of almost 50 years earlier. Big Bing CV carbs helped give the 745cc pushrod motor a peak output of 50 BHP. Right: Brochure photo suggests that motorcycling clothing has changed more since the early Seventies than have the bikes themselves.

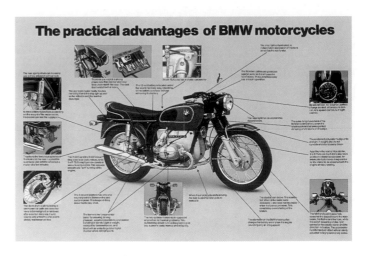

The practical advantages of BMW motorcycles

marque had become known. The new frame had a single large-diameter top tube and twin downtubes, which curved upwards just behind the engine, giving a look similar to that of Norton's Featherbed.

The engine retained the basic layout of air-cooled, two-valves-per-cylinder, pushrod-operated flat twin. But the /5-series unit was completely new and larger, as its tall top section incorporated an electric starter and air filter housing. The R75/5 had a capacity of 745cc and produced 50 BHP at 6200 RPM, giving a 10 BHP advantage over the 599cc R60/5. All three motors shared innovations, including alloy cylinder barrels, strengthened transmission, smaller flywheel, and one-piece forged crankshaft with plain instead of roller bearings.

With these models BMW was making an effort to broaden its appeal by attracting more sporting riders, so the bikes were offered in a choice of colors, rather than just the traditional black or occasional white. In 1972, when this bike was built, the firm went even farther by introducing a smaller, 18-liter tank, complete with chromed side panels and matching shiny battery covers.

The "toaster tank" proved too extravagant for most BMW riders, and was dropped the next year. But on a dull day it added a bit of sparkle to this clean and original boxer, which came quickly to life at a press of the button on the narrow handlebars. The crankshaft's torque-reaction lurch to one side was barely noticeable, and first gear went in with less of a clonk than I'd expected. But the bike still felt every bit a BMW boxer as I pulled away, its rear end rising in characteristic shaft-drive fashion.

Back in 1969, the R75/5 had been unusual in its use of constant vacuum carburetors; even the smaller /5 models had made do with conventional carbs. The 32 mm Bings still worked well, giving the BMW a pleasantly flexible feel as I accelerated away, with no sign of the heavy throttle action that was criticized in one contemporary magazine test. There was enough low-down torque that I didn't need to keep an eye on the small tachometer in the bottom of the speedo.

At slow speeds the 75/5's manners were every bit as good as might be expected of such an aristocratic and expensive machine. Lack of leverage on the narrow handlebars meant the steering felt rather heavy, but in traffic my only real complaint was that the nonstandard crashbars combined with the sticking-out cylinders' big Bing carbs to get in the way when I put a foot down at a standstill.

BMW R75/5 (1972)

Engine type	Air-cooled pushrod, 2-valve horizontally opposed twin
Displacement	745cc
Bore x stroke	82 x 70.6 mm
Compression ratio	9:1
Carburetion	2 x 32 mm Bing CVs
Claimed power	50 BHP @ 6200 RPM
Transmission	4-speed
Electrics	12 V battery
Frame	Tubular steel cradle
Front suspension	Telescopic, no adjustment
Rear suspension	Twin shock absorbers, adjustable preload
Front brake	200 mm (8 in) TLS drum
Rear brake	200 mm (8 in) SLS drum
Front tire	3.25 x 19 in
Rear tire	4.00 x 18 in
Wheelbase	1384 mm (54.5 in)
Seat height	851 mm (34 in)
Fuel capacity	18 liters (4 UK, 4.7 US gal)
Weight	190 kg (418 lb) dry

The BMW was respectably light at 190 kg (418 lb), which helped make it quick off the mark. Its 0–60 mph (97 km/h) time was less than six seconds, impressive at the time, and it rumbled through the standing quarter in fourteen seconds, heading for a top speed of about 110 mph (176 km/h). At most engine speeds the engine was very smooth, too. Although the gearbox had only four speeds, with quite a gap between third and fourth, the BMW sat at an indicated 80 mph (129 km/h) with an ease that suggested it could do so all day long.

In bends the 75/5 lived up to the German marque's reputation for reliable if less than sporty handling. Despite their long travel, the gaitered front forks were quite well damped and didn't dive as much as I'd expected when I gave the reasonably powerful twin-leading-shoe front drum brake a good

squeeze. Although the shocks were quite soft, they worked well, especially when I wound on some extra preload using the useful levers at the bottom of each spring.

Once into a turn the twin held its line well and felt pleasantly planted, though care had to be taken not to cause the shaft-drive rear end to move down by closing the throttle, especially as this bike's crash-bars scraped long before the narrow Metzeler tires ran out of grip. More than its cornering speed, though, it was the BMW's practicality and long-distance comfort that endeared it to the minority of motorcyclists fortunate enough to be able to afford one.

It's arguable that those refinements gave the BMW an edge even over Honda's CB750, still the superbike yardstick in 1972. The German bike was not perfect. Its pillion footrests were too close to the silencers, resulting in some burned boot heels; and the indicator switch was illogically designed and located on the right handlebar. (Some things haven't changed at BMW.) But overall the 75/5's blend of performance, handling, comfort, and build quality meant that if you had distance to travel at speed and in style, few bikes even came close to matching it.

Right: The R75/5 had a new twin-downtube steel frame with Norton Featherbed-style curved tubes at the top rear. The flat-twin engine layout, with the crankshaft running along the line of the bike, made shaft final drive an obvious solution. Excellent fuel economy combined with reasonable tank capacity to give a generous range.

From *Bike*, Winter 1972

"BMW have gone to great lengths to give their new machines a sportier image in an effort to carve a bigger slice of the US market, and weight reduction was obviously high on their list of priorities.

The BMW could be aimed into slow corners more in the style of a Norton and had power all through the range, which would pull you round without judder or gasp. But heavy throttle action (those vacuum carbs?) made screwing it on a carefully considered exercise... Accelerating out of corners, or anyplace else come to that, was a total blast... power came on strong as an ox.

The term 'Rolls-Royce of motorcycles' has oft been applied to the BMW; since the factory revamped the bike and gave it more go and less weight, if pushed into making analogies I would prefer instead to refer to it as the Jaguar XJ6."

Suzuki GT750J

It appeared one morning like a vehicle from outer space—big, bright, and impossibly glamorous. I was fiddling with my bicycle in the street outside my house, aged about 13, when I looked up to see a huge pink motorbike pull up at the side of the road. Its rider killed the engine and called out to me for directions to a local dealership.

I just about managed to blurt out the route before, with a word of thanks, a nod, and a brief wave of leather-gloved hand, he accelerated rapidly away, leaving behind a crisp, burbling exhaust note, a haze of two-stroke smoke, and one very wide-eyed teenager. It was quite an exit. And the GT750 was one very impressive motorbike.

Back then in the early Seventies, the two-stroke triple was one of the most glamorous bikes on the road, and one of the biggest as well. Suzuki's first superbike was powered by an engine that was essentially one-and-a-half units from the air-cooled T500 twin. Keeping the same 70 x 64 mm cylinder dimensions, but adding an extra cylinder plus liquid cooling, resulted in a 739cc triple that produced a maximum of 67 BHP at 6500 RPM.

The GT750 was a very different machine from the competent and quick, but small and rather forgettable, T500. In the car world the letters GT stood for Gran Turismo—signifying performance with comfort and style—and Suzuki set out to build a two-wheeled equivalent. The GT750 they produced was a true grand tourer of its day: big, soft, and reasonably fast, but with the emphasis more on refinement than pure speed. It was about as different from Kawasaki's raw and aggressive air-cooled H2 as another two-stroke triple could be.

Chassis-wise the GT750 was conventional, with twin-down-tube frame, gaitered front forks, preload-adjustable twin shocks, and drum brakes at both ends. But the Suzuki looked like nothing else on the road, with its big radiator—complete with chromed

Opposite: Suzuki's 739cc liquid-cooled two-stroke triple was smooth, softly tuned and like no other motorcycle engine. Above: Bulbous styling and vivid pink paintwork ensured that the GT750 stood out from the crowd. Right: This bike's double twin-leading-shoe front drum brake lacked power, making it easy to understand why Suzuki changed to a twin disc set-up in 1973.

crash-bar around its edge, smooth liquid-cooled cylinders, and black-tipped reverse-cone silencers. Most of all, this very clean and original GT750J sported vivid pink paintwork totally in keeping with its 1972 vintage.

I felt as though I should have been wearing a tank top and flared trousers as I threw a leg over the Suzuki's broad saddle and hit the button to send the motor burbling into life. The riding position was upright, hands reaching up to highish bars and feet well forward in touring style. The bike's weight and tall seat made it a bit of a handful at a standstill, but the engine's crisp response from very low revs made the bike easy to ride once I was under way.

Its 67 BHP peak output was nothing special (Honda had claimed an identical output for the CB750 back in 1969, after all) but the GT750 certainly scored with refinement, low-rev torque, and smoothness, if not with top-end clout. The Suzuki pulled so effort-

Specifications:
Maximum Speed: 120–125mph, Maximum Horsepower: 70.0bp/6,500rpm S.A.E. NET, Engine Type: 2-stroke, liquid cooled, 3-cylinder, Transmission: 5-speed, constant mesh, Lubrication: Suzuki CCI, Overall Length: 2,205mm (86.8in), Overall Width: 880mm (34.6in), Overall Height: 1,125mm (44.3in), Ground Clearance: 140mm (5.5in), Suspension, Front: Telescopic, oil-dampened, Rear: Oil-dampened, 5-way adjustable, Starter: Electric and kick.

Suzuki GT750J (1972)

Engine type	Liquid-cooled two-stroke transverse triple
Displacement	738cc
Bore x stroke	70 x 64 mm
Compression ratio	N/A
Carburetion	3 x 32 mm Mikuni
Claimed power	67 BHP @ 6500 RPM
Transmission	5-speed
Electrics	12-volt battery
Frame	Tubular steel cradle
Front suspension	Telescopic, no adjustment
Rear suspension	Twin shock absorbers, adjustable preload
Front brake	Twin-sided 200 mm (8 in) TLS drum
Rear brake	180 mm (7 in) SLS drum
Front tire	3.25 x 19 in
Rear tire	4.00 x 18 in
Wheelbase	1473 mm (58 in)
Seat height	813 mm (32 in)
Fuel capacity	17 liters (3.75 UK gal, 4.5 US gal)
Weight	238 kg (524 lb) wet

lessly, even when its tachometer needle was barely above the 2000 RPM mark, that it was easy to understand why many contemporary testers had raved about its power delivery despite its less-than-dramatic high-rev acceleration.

The rubber-mounted, 120-degree triple engine was remarkably smooth at almost all speeds, adding to its air of refinement by also being very quiet, at least in comparison to its almost exclusively air-cooled contemporaries. This bike's refined feel was marred slightly by the clouds of exhaust smoke that it spewed out, though it had the excuse that the oil pump had been set high because the recently rebuilt motor was not fully run-in.

If anything, being unable to rev the GT to its red-line was a bonus, as I would probably have been disappointed had I done so. The big stroker cruised along very happily at 70 mph (115 km/h), indicating only about 4500 RPM, and was happy to up the pace to

From *Cycle World*, Dec. 1971

"Big, heavy, comfortable, economical and extremely smooth, the T750 is capable of high 13-sec standing start quarter-miles, effortless high speed cruising, hairline steering and tremendous braking. It's a Superbike in every sense of the word.

Like the T500, the GT750 gets top marks in the handling department... Even under hard acceleration in high-speed corners, the GT750 tracked as though on rails... The Suzuki's shocks are very sensitive to small road irregularities, and have sufficient damping to prevent rear wheel hop under heavy braking, or yawing in fast corners.

Riding the GT750 is a joy that must be experienced to be fully appreciated. The wide, ultra-soft dual seat is very comfortable, although we had a heavy friend who complained that the padding was too soft. Suzuki's most pleasing combination, the GT750 is the most refined, and yet most awesome, two-stroke ever."

about 90 mph (145 km/h) for a short burst. Even when fully run-in it would have begun to get a bit breathless shortly afterwards, before reaching a top speed of about 110 mph (176 km/h).

Having set out expecting the Suzuki's handling to be slow and heavy enough to justify the "water buffalo" nickname that the bike had in the States (in Britain it was always simply the "kettle"), I was pleasantly surprised to find that it was not as bad as I'd feared. Sure, if I attacked a bend in a remotely aggressive fashion, the big bike's soft and under-damped suspension combined with its weight to introduce a distinct wallowing motion, and ground clearance was very limited.

But I wasn't about to treat this elderly machine too harshly, and at a more relaxed pace the GT750 was very well behaved and even respectably agile. It certainly wasn't a bike on which I'd have gone out looking for a twisty road, but it was capable of providing some entertainment when it came across one. Even if those soft and spindly front forks meant that I had to slow to the right speed, then drive through the turn in the approved fashion, rather than brake into the bend and risk a wobble from the over-stressed front end.

The brakes themselves were distinctly mediocre, despite the front stopper consisting of a serious-looking pair of twin-leading-shoe drums. One contemporary test described the GT's brakes as "just short of fantastic," so maybe this bike's lack of stopping power was due to the drums and shoes needing fine-tuning. But it's probably no coincidence that one of the first updates Suzuki made, in 1973, was to fit the GT750K with a twin-disc front end.

Further updates followed in each of the next three years, including taller overall gearing, various carb and exhaust changes, plus the addition of a gear indicator in the instrument console. The most significant revision came with the 1975-model GT750M, which produced 70 BHP, a gain of 3 BHP, thanks largely to increased compression ratio.

Despite that, the GT750 never quite lost its reputation for

being slightly dull, especially alongside the manic Kawasaki Mach IV with which it was sometimes rather unfairly compared. Like its rival Japanese two-stroke triple, Suzuki's big all-rounder faded away toward the end of the decade, a victim of increasingly tight emissions laws. All these years later, though, the GT750J's lurid paintwork, bulbous shape, and clouds of exhaust smoke make it in many ways the ultimate two-wheeled symbol of the early Seventies.

Moto Guzzi V7 Sport

This is getting hectic. Ahead of me is the bright red shape of an Alfa Romeo saloon car being driven rapidly down a winding country road. Behind it, I am gunning the Guzzi's V-twin engine for all it's worth, then squeezing the brake lever hard and hurling the bike through the bends in an attempt to keep up. And on every straight I'm lifting my left hand off the bars to prevent my loose-fitting goggles from slipping off altogether.

My increasingly desperate attempts to keep up with the Alfa are not designed just to prove that two-wheeled Italian vehicles are faster than four-wheeled ones, even when ridden one-handed and watery-eyed. Quite simply, the driver is my photographer, he knows where he's going and I don't—so I'm very keen not to lose him. Besides, sometimes it's nice to have an incentive to ride hard, especially when you are riding a bike like this immaculately restored Guzzi V7 Sport, without doubt one of the best early-Seventies machines that I could have chosen for the chase. The Sport fully deserved its name, as this breakthrough model for Guzzi was the first truly sporting machine to be built using the Mandello del Lario firm's transverse V-twin engine.

Opposite: The Sport's top-quality cycle parts included Guzzi's own front forks, Borrani alloy wheel rims and a big twin-leading-shoe front drum brake. Above: Lean, green, and among the fastest bikes on the road in the early Seventies. Right: Removing the dynamo in the Vee of previous V-twins allowed a much more compact frame design.

The V7 Sport was introduced in 1971, after Guzzi engineer Lino Tonti had produced a new frame to house a new 90-degree transverse V-twin motor developed from that of the less racy V7 Special. Guzzi's trademark engine had originally been designed in the late Fifties to power the 3x3, a tractor-like device produced for the Italian ministry of defense. Guzzi, looking for a replacement for its ageing Falcone flat-single, had then upgraded the shaft-drive V-twin to power police bikes and the 703cc V7 tourer of 1967.

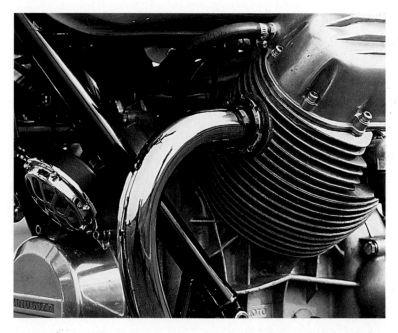

when the seat was lifted.

This immaculate Sport dates from 1973, being one of the last of fewer than 4000 that were produced before production ended toward the end of that year. It certainly felt exotic, strange even, as I climbed aboard and fired up the engine—which can be done either with the starter button or, in car style, by turning the ignition key—to feel that trademark lurch to the right of the longitudinal crankshaft.

For V7 Sport use, the touring motor was made more powerful and compact. Bore and stroke dimensions of 82.5 x 70 mm gave capacity of 748cc, reduced from the 757cc of earlier models (including the V7 Special), allowing entry in 750cc races. Valve gear and conrods were lightened, and twin coils and points fitted along with bigger, 30 mm Dell'Orto carbs. The result was a peak output of 52 BHP at 6400 RPM, well up on the touring engine's 40 BHP.

There were plenty of changes in the bottom end, too, although the new motor retained old-style features such as the simple gauze strainer, instead of a proper oil filter. A new, heavily ribbed crankcase and five-speed gearbox were added, and a more compact Bosch alternator situated on the front of the crank replaced the previous motor's large car-type dynamo between the cylinders.

Tonti's frame was lower than its predecessors due to its top rails (which were strengthened by a diagonal spine) running between the cylinders, where the dynamo had previously been. Its front forks contained sealed damper units. Wheels were 18-inchers, the front holding a big 220 mm (8.7 in) double-sided twin-leading-shoe front drum brake.

Guzzi certainly knew how to build an eye-catching motorbike in those days. As well as the lime-green paintwork, the first 150 examples of the V7 had bright red frames. Numerous neat details included the "swan-neck" clip-on handlebars that could be slid up the forks to give an upright riding position. Under the seat was a small inspection light that automatically illuminated

This bike's bars were set in the normal, lowest position so the riding position was stretched forward and sporty. As I pulled away I was conscious of the way the engine's low-rev shaking smoothed as the revs rose, noise increasing with a blend of hollow sucking from the Dell'Ortos and muffled bark from the stylish but rather too efficient (at least for my liking) Silentium pipes.

Guzzi V-twins have a reputation for low-revving torque, but the V7's 750cc motor really came alive only at about 4500 RPM, and pulled strongly from there to the red-line at 7250 RPM. At lower revs it ran perfectly well, but it didn't generate much in the way of forward motion when I wound open the Tomaselli twistgrip.

Provided the motor was kept spinning, though, life was much more interesting. The Guzzi showed a healthy turn of acceleration, even from speeds of 70 mph (113 km/h) and above, and cruised at 90 mph (145 km/h) plus with an effortless feel. If I slid back on the

Moto Guzzi V7 Sport (1973)

Engine type	Air-cooled pushrod, 2-valve transverse V-twin
Displacement	748cc
Bore x stroke	82.5 x 70 mm
Compression ratio	9.8:1
Carburetion	2 x 30 mm Dell'Ortos
Claimed power	52hp @ 6300 RPM at rear wheel
Transmission	5-speed
Electrics	12 V battery
Frame	Tubular steel spine/twin cradle
Front suspension	Telescopic, no adjustment
Rear suspension	Twin shock absorbers, adjustable preload
Front brake	Twin 220 mm (8.7 in) TLS drum
Rear brake	220 mm (8.7 in) TLS drum
Front tire	90/90 x 18 in
Rear tire	110/90 x 18 in
Wheelbase	1470 mm (57.9 in)
Seat height	730 mm (28.7 in)
Fuel capacity	22 liters (4.8 UK gal, 5.8 US gal)
Weight	225 kg (495 lb) wet

From *Motorcyclist*, Dec. 1972

"When riding the V7 Sport you can feel the immediate and complete security of a machine which follows the pilot in each movement even when pushing it at high speed on curvy roads.

All this enthusiasm for a motorcycle derives from a fundamental fact which you can feel while riding it. It has exceptionally good handling and stability because it is so compact and has such a low layout.

Although the V7 Sport has sporting features it can be used for touring and long trips without tiring the rider. This is due not only to the aforementioned characteristics but to some less noticeable features such as an engine that does not wobble, plus sturdy suspension. The V7 Sport is really a motorcycle which means something in today's motorcycle world, and even if the price is a little high it will surely be accepted by two-wheeled enthusiasts everywhere."

seat and tucked my knees in as the designer intended, the Sport loped along at an indicated 100 mph (160 km/h), with plenty of speed in hand to its 125 mph (200 km/h) top speed.

Stability was always a Guzzi strength, and the V7 stayed solid both in a straight line and in fast curves, thanks in no small part to the rigidity of its frame, which used the big V-twin engine as a stressed member. Suspension was good, too, although the front forks were rather soft and underdamped, and their sealed hydraulic damper units meant that this could not easily be cured by using thicker oil in the normal fashion.

Despite weighing 225 kg (495 lb) the Sport could be flicked around quite easily, and its handling did not suffer too much from the shaft-drive rear end. This bike's Bridgestone tires gave reassuringly modern levels of grip, too. Apart from an occasional squeal at low speed, there was not much wrong with the big double twin-leading-shoe drum brake, which gave plenty of bite even at high speed. My only chassis-related concern was that the gearlever grounded, with potentially disastrous consequences, when well cranked over to the right.

That didn't prevent the lime-green machine from being a pretty quick bike, as the driver of that much younger Alfa discovered. The V7 Sport was too expensive to sell in big numbers but it established Guzzi as a manufacturer of high-class sporting superbikes. No wonder the Mandello firm honored it by releasing the similarly styled V11 Sport in 1999. The V7 Sport is where the legend of big, fast Moto Guzzi V-twins began.

Triumph X-75 Hurricane

Has there ever been a production motorcycle as cool as Triumph's X-75 Hurricane? Leaning on its sidestand, sunlight reflecting off the chrome of its trio of exhaust pipes, and the wasp-waisted tank-seat unit emphasizing the handsome air-cooled motor, the Hurricane looks far too stylish and futuristic to have been produced in the early Seventies by a BSA-Triumph firm in deep financial trouble.

Its looks were by no means the only thing for which the X-75 was memorable, either. The Triumph's 60 BHP engine, a lower-geared version of the T150 Trident/BSA Rocket 3 unit, made this one of the quickest-accelerating bikes on the roads back in 1973. Given the Hurricane's style, performance, and rarity—fewer than 1200 were ever built—it's no surprise that it is among the best-loved of Seventies classics.

For any cynics wondering how the ailing British industry managed to come up with a bike as neat as the Hurricane, there's a simple answer—this bike was designed without Triumph's Meriden factory bosses even knowing about it. The X-75 was shaped not in Britain but in America—in top secret, by young freelance designer Craig Vetter.

Opposite: High bars and tiny tank were not very practical, but few owners minded. Above: The X-75's profile is one of the most distinctive in all motorcycling, and one of the most attractive, too. Right: The Hurricane could be persuaded to go around corners, but in general it preferred straight roads.

The whole concept of the X-75 originated in the States, with Don Brown, the vice chairman of BSA's American company. When the original Trident and Rocket 3 triples were revealed in late 1968, US market reaction was very poor, mainly because of the bikes' angular styling. "The only way we were going to sell the triples was by re-styling them, I was convinced of that," Brown later recalled.

Brown approached Vetter, who ran a business making fairings and had just displayed two bikes of his own design at a show in Daytona. It was agreed that the project would be kept secret even from the BSA Group's chairman, and Vetter was provided with a standard Rocket 3 on which to start work. His prototype retained

the BSA's angled-forward, 740cc pushrod engine and twin-down-tube steel frame, but Vetter extended the cylinder head fins to make the motor look bigger and more impressive. (Special heads were machined for production versions.)

Almost every other part of the triple was modified or changed. The handlebars were higher, clocks were mounted above a new chromed headlight, and front forks were lengthened by 50 mm (two in). The wheels comprised polished hubs, chromed spokes, and alloy rims, holding a 19-inch front tire and a fatter 18-inch rear. Three exhaust downpipes slanted across the front of the motor, and then ran back to the bank of shiny, upswept silencers on the right side.

Best of all, the original slab-sided bodywork was replaced by a slender and graceful fiberglass form that blended the fuel tank into the side panel area, above which was a dual-seat with a chromed pillion grab rail. The tiny gas tank was undeniably impractical, but the visual effect was stunning.

Despite the secrecy surrounding the project, the American BSA firm's president Peter Thornton heard about the prototype and asked Vetter to bring it to New Jersey. The reaction was so posi-tive that Thornton had the bike shipped to Meriden the same day—complete with instructions that it was to be built with no changes. BSA's subsequent financial collapse ensured that the triples, all assembled between June 1972 and January 1973, were marketed as the Triumph X-75 Hurricane.

From the pilot's seat the handlebars seem more wide than high, giving a bolt-upright riding position with feet placed well forward. The ignition is on the left, below the steering head. There's no electric start but, given a gentle prod of the kick-start, the triple burst into life with a pleasant three-cylinder warbling from its side-by-side silencers.

Right: Those three mufflers gave a glorious wail as the three-cylinder engine approached its peak at 7250rpm. Below: The production X-75 looked very like Craig Vetter's original prototype, which was commissioned and designed in the States without the knowledge of BSA's bosses. Its 740cc triple engine sat with cylinders angled forward like that of BSA's Rocket 3, rather than upright like Triumph's similar Trident unit.

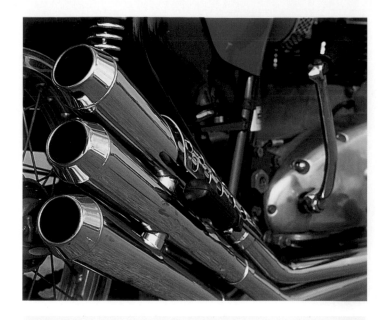

Triumph's old three-cylinder motor was always regarded as smooth, and that was certainly true of this lovingly restored machine. The triple traditionally likes to be revved, too, but the Hurricane pulled fairly well from low revs, kicking harder above 4000 RPM and emitting a wonderful exhaust wail as the revs rose toward the peak power figure of 7250 RPM.

The impression of acceleration in the lower gears was terrific by Seventies standards, thanks to the Hurricane's blend of exposed riding position, relatively light weight, and short gearing. I had plenty of opportunity to practice my right-foot change on the five-speed Triumph, whose top speed of about 115 mph (185 km/h) was 10 mph (16 km/h) down on that of the T150 Trident, due to the gearing—although its standing quarter-mile time of just over 13 seconds was at least half a second quicker.

Triumph X-75 Hurricane (1973)

Engine type	Air-cooled pushrod, 6-valve transverse triple
Displacement	740cc
Bore x stroke	67 x 70 mm
Compression ratio	9:1
Carburetion	3 x 27 mm Amals
Claimed power	60 BHP @ 7250 RPM
Transmission	5-speed
Electrics	12 V battery
Frame	Tubular steel twin cradle
Front suspension	Telescopic, no adjustment
Rear suspension	Twin shock absorbers, adjustable preload
Front brake	203 mm (8 in) TLS drum
Rear brake	178 mm (7 in) SLS drum
Front tire	3.25 x 19 in
Rear tire	4.25 x 18 in
Wheelbase	1524 mm (60 in)
Seat height	825 mm (32.5 in)
Fuel capacity	10 liters (2.2 UK gal, 2.6 US gal)
Weight	191 kg (420 lb) dry

For gentle use the bike was comfortable, thanks partly to the generous seat and the fact that vibration only became noticeable, mainly through the handlebars, above about 5000 RPM. But at higher speeds it was a different story. Performance began to tail off at about 90 mph (145 km/h), and wind pressure meant that few riders would have wanted to hold that speed for long.

The Triumph's handling traditionally also discouraged high-speed riding, because the X-75 earned a dubious reputation thanks to its combination of high handlebars, kicked-out forks, and ribbed front tire. But this bike remained stable, and delivered a fairly sporty ride thanks to firm shocks and front forks that, although long, were reasonably well damped.

Its conical, twin-leading-shoe drum front brake gave a rather soft feel at the lever but pulled the Triumph up reasonably well, in conjunction with the smaller rear drum. Even so, the X-75 would have benefited from the single disc brake that Triumph

Below: Even Vetter's sharp lines can't make the left side look as good as the right. The pillion grab-rail was useful because the three-cylinder engine's power and short gearing gave the X-75 fearsome acceleration. The Triumph's 18-inch diameter rear tire was wider than the 19-inch ribbed front, enhancing the custom look. Firm rear shocks did not prevent some instability at high speed.

introduced on the T150V Trident in 1973.

In the end, though, the X-75 wasn't so much about performance as about style and attitude. The more conventional Trident was in many respects a better all-around performer—faster, more stable, better braked, more comfortable at speed, and with better fuel range—but the Hurricane had the looks and the low-speed acceleration that made it more popular with some riders, despite a higher price tag.

Craig Vetter went on to become famous for his fairings and luggage systems. But as long as the Triumph X-75 Hurricane is ridden and admired, its designer will be remembered as the man who brought a touch of American glitz to the classic British triple.

From *Motorcyclist*, Apr. 1973

"Custom design wizard Craig Vetter was brought in on the case and given the task of transforming an everyday road bike into an all-American café racer. Like Doctor Jekyll transforming into Mr. Hyde, the Rocket Three was molded into the Hurricane.

The obvious cosmetic design features are novel and certainly attractive. There's no doubt that the Hurricane is the most striking machine ever offered by Triumph. Vetter's two most obvious styling changes are the fiberglass seat/tank cowling and the upswept exhaust system on the right side of the machine.

Resembling very much the exhaust system used on the Honda 350 Six road racers, the café racer–styled three pipes and mufflers are both eye and ear appealing. There's absolutely no question that the Hurricane has the sweetest exhaust note in town. It's a harmonic exhaust tone that makes the hair stand up on the back of your neck when riding on mountain roads. You don't even have to get out of second gear to feel like Romero or Nixon."

Ducati 750 Sport

Without the traffic it would be a brilliant biking route. The road snakes and dips through the countryside, a narrow two-lane ribbon whose many bends offer a challenging variety of angles, cambers, and speeds. It's Ducati Country, to quote the famous advertising phrase—except that today there are far too many trucks, each one droning slowly along at the head of a long line of cars.

But it's still a great ride on the 750 Sport, which dispatches the traffic almost as though it wasn't there. Every time I catch up to a line of vehicles, the slim Ducati zips past, barely needing to use the opposite side of the road as it picks them off one by one. The bike's stability is impressive, its instant reaction to an occasional touch of brake reassuring, and its effortless acceleration hugely satisfying.

The 750 Sport's pace and efficiency on that busy road came as some surprise, because early Ducati V-twins are normally revered more for their speed through fast curves than their ability to cut through traffic. Although this Sport's handling didn't disappoint, it

Opposite: Clip-on handlebars, yellow paintwork, and big V-twin engine were the Sport's key features. Above: The Ducati's racy profile incorporated a single seat and left no doubt about this bike's purpose. Right: Brochure shot suggests that the earlier GT750 model's pillion seat might sometimes be more useful than extra horsepower.

Ducati

MECCANICA S.p.A.
Via A.C. Ducati, 3 - Cas. Post. 313 - 40100 Bologna - Italia
Tel. (051) 40.50.49 - Telex 51492

The Sport's basic chassis components were also shared with the GT, including the steel frame that was a larger version of the trellis designed for Ducati's 500cc V-twin racers by British specialist Colin Seeley. Marzocchi supplied leading-axle forks and rear shocks; braking was handled by a single 280 mm (11 in) front disc, with a single-leading-shoe drum at the rear.

Where the Sport chassis differed was in its clip-on handlebars, rear-set footpegs and single seat, plus a half-fairing in some markets. The Sport's other most obvious difference was its yellow tank and side panels, in contrast to the restrained red and black of the GT. This bike just looks *right*, its bold paintwork complementing the heavily finned motor and slender Conti pipes. There's no starter motor, no indicators, no excess weight.

That's great once you're moving, although the high-compression motor needs a hefty kick before it will roar into life. The bars are low and well forward, but the footpegs are not radically rear-set, giving a rather hunched riding position that leaves knees and elbows in close proximity. The clutch is light; first gear goes in with

was the motor's flexibility that made even more of a lasting impression.

This bike's V-twin engine is not a desmo, either. Back in 1973, Ducati had yet to introduce desmodromic valve gear for roadsters. But the Sport, whose single overhead cams operate valves closed by conventional coil springs, is an important model in Ducati history. Lean, aggressive, and functional, the 750 was the Bologna factory's first true sporting V-twin.

Essentially the 750 Sport was a racer version of the 750GT, Ducati's first big V-twin, which had been introduced two years earlier by the firm then best known for elegant singles. Engineer Fabio Taglioni's design established the 90-degree air-cooled layout, with dimensions of 80 x 74.4 mm giving a capacity of 748cc. The GT's peak output of 50 BHP was raised to 56 BHP at 8200 RPM for the Sport, by a higher 9:1 compression ratio, plus larger 32 mm Dell'Orto carburetors that were filterless apart from wire mesh over the end of each bellmouth.

Ducati 750

a gentle, right-footed nudge on the one-up, four-down gearbox. And then the Sport is accelerating away, its midrange torque and light weight doing much to compensate for the lack of outright horsepower.

My first impression of the engine was of how tractable and eager it was. Throttle response was excellent at virtually any speed, a crack of the right wrist prompting the Dell'Ortos' accelerator pumps to deliver a dollop of straight juice that sent the Ducati barreling forward. The gears snicked in easily, and the 750's flexibility meant that on a fairly fast road there was rarely any need to come

down more than one ratio for all but the tightest of bends.

Some vibration came drumming through the bars and seat from about 70 mph (113 km/h), giving a reminder that the sparsely padded Sport was too single-minded to be comfortable on long runs. Even so, the 750 cruised with a fairly unstressed and long-legged feel. Revved harder, it would produce useful power to the 8000 RPM red zone, with a top speed of about 125 mph (200 km/h)—good enough to show a clean pair of Contis to most bikes in 1973.

That was especially true when a few bends were added, for it was then that the Ducati's lightness and chassis quality showed their worth. Aided by braided hose, this bike's cast-iron single disc and Lockheed caliper hauled the Sport up efficiently—hard enough that I didn't feel the need for the second disc that was originally an optional extra.

And although the Marzocchis at either end didn't provide much comfort, the suspension and frame coped well with hard cornering. With the V-twin's lengthy 1500 mm (59 in) wheelbase and a 19-inch front wheel, the Sport was never going to be particularly agile.

Ducati 750 Sport (1973)

Engine type	Air-cooled SOHC, 2-valve 90-degree V-twin
Displacement	748cc
Bore x stroke	80 x 74.4 mm
Compression ratio	9:1
Carburetion	2 x 32 mm Dell'Ortos
Claimed power	56 BHP @ 8200 RPM
Transmission	5-speed
Electrics	12 V battery; 45/40 W headlamp
Frame	Tubular steel
Front suspension	Marzocchi leading-link telescopic, no adjustment
Rear suspension	Twin Marzocchi shock absorbers, adjustable preload
Front brake	Single 280 mm (11 in) disc; second disc optional extra
Rear brake	203 mm (8 in) SLS drum
Front tire	3.25 x 19 in
Rear tire	4.10 x 18 in
Wheelbase	1500 mm (59 in)
Seat height	790 mm (31 in)
Fuel capacity	20 liters (4.4 UK gal, 5.3 US gal)
Weight	195 kg (429 lb) dry

Below: The 750 Sport's successor was the 750SS, first of the long line of Super Sport models. Inspired by Paul Smart's victory in the 1972 Imola 200-mile race, the 750SS was introduced in the following year. It featured a half fairing, single seat, and tuned engine with desmodromic valvegear. In 1975 the engine was enlarged to 864cc to create the 900SS (featured on page 108).

But it could be made to change direction precisely and even quickly, given a firm nudge on the narrow clip-ons.

On bumpy roads, the Sport bounced around a bit as the stiff and crudely damped units failed to react fast enough. But this bike's Dunlop TT100s gave plenty of grip, ground clearance was generous, and it was easy to imagine how a hard-charging Ducati pilot could have embarrassed riders of more powerful bikes.

Despite this and the publicity boost from Paul Smart's famous win in the Imola 200 race in April 1972, the expensive and impractical Sport was not a huge success for Ducati. Production was halted at the end of 1974, after a few specification changes, including new forks and switchgear. A year later the Sport was softened with a dual seat and pillion footrests in a belated attempt to attract a wider audience.

Partly because of its comparative rarity, the 750 Sport is now a very desirable model—and why not, indeed? With its classical lines, gorgeous sound, exhilarating performance, and purposeful character, the aptly named Sport was the model that heralded a string of magical V-twins from Ducati.

From *Cycle*, JAN. 1973

"The seat padding and the riding position automatically disqualify the Sport for long-distance hauling. It's strictly a Walter Mitty Speciale, built for honking hard along back-country roads. At this task the machine is simply superb.

The controls operate crisply, and there is a one-to-one feeling of correspondence between the rider and the machine parts. The clip-ons and rear-sets—combined with the excellent handling and Dunlop TT100 tires—add to the fun of the countryside swervery.

But the racer get-up intensifies the low-speed heaviness in the Ducati's handling. In short, stay out of town, and that's not such a bad thing anyway if John Law in your hometown takes exception to those 90dB(A) notes pouring out of the pipes.

One thing is certain. The Sport is not just a showpiece. It is quickly establishing its credentials as a first-rate flyer."

mod. 750 SS
CONSUMO 16 Km./litro*
* norme CUNA

MV Agusta 750 Sport

I am sitting at the traffic lights, blipping the throttle and savoring the cacophony of whirring gears and barking exhaust from this most deliciously noisy of bikes. The MV has no mirrors, so I don't realize that there's another bike behind me—until, immediately as the lights change, a modern middleweight comes storming past, its rider clearly aiming to put this old machine in its place.

On most Seventies bikes I'd let him go. But not this one. MV Agusta honor is at stake, so I wrench back the 750 Sport's throttle and bury my head behind the screen. The feeling of raw, race-bred aggression is magical as the four-cylinder engine reaches 5500 RPM and kicks hard with a spine-tingling bellow from its quartet of pipes.

Moments later I'm traveling at about 90 mph (145 km/h), still accelerating, then treading into top gear as the Sport closes the gap slightly. As we approach a sweeping right-hander I'm right with him. The MV remains rock solid as I brush its front brake lever, then dial in the throttle again to keep the bike driving through.

Another brief, deafening burst of acceleration follows on the next straight, and the gap is unchanged as we brake for the following roundabout. The MV's twin front discs bite, slowing the bike hard despite its skinny front tire. Then, as quickly as it began, the duel is over. My opponent turns off at the first exit while I carry on round, with no time to continue the chase.

If there is one Seventies bike on which a challenge is hard to ignore, it's MV Agusta's 750 Sport. With its racy lines and its fire-breathing four-cylinder engine, this is a street-legal development of one of the greatest racebikes of all time. In 1973, when this 750 Sport was being assembled at the Agusta base in Gallarate, near Milan, Phil Read was winning the firm's 16th consecutive 500cc

Opposite: Along with a striking red, white, and blue paint scheme, the Sport carried an MV logo whose cog design was appropriate, given the engine's gear-driven cams. Above: Full fairing, clip-on bars, and red seat made the ultimate race-replica even more special. Right: The race-developed four-cylinder engine featured sand-cast cases and distinctive twin-cam layout.

Its engine was based on that of the 600, having 7 mm wider pistons giving a capacity of 743cc. A higher compression ratio, larger exhaust valves, and four instead of two 24 mm Dell'Orto carbs lifted peak output to 65 BHP at 7900 RPM. Like the competition unit, it featured gear-driven twin overhead cams. The race engine had no generator, so a combined starter/dynamo sat beneath the engine, connected by two belts.

Surprisingly the Sport retained the 600's shaft final drive and also its frame, which had a single top tube instead of twin tubes like the racers. Ceriani provided the twin rear shocks and 35 mm front forks; the 600's feeble (if innovative) front disc brake was replaced by a big four-leading-shoe Grimeca drum.

This bike is essentially a 1973 model machine, upgraded with the twin-disc front end that was introduced later that year. At that time the engine gained higher compression (10:1) pistons, reshaped cylinder head, larger inlet valves, and 27 mm carbs, increasing peak output to 69 BHP. The Brembo front brake calipers are as fitted on later bikes. Its full fairing was a factory option, as were a half-fairing and flyscreen.

From the tall saddle you stretch across the shapely fuel tank with its badge signifying MV's record number of 36 world championship wins. Ahead are a tall screen, black-faced Smiths instruments, and a simple pair of warning lights. Reach down to tickle the Dell'Ortos, then press the button in the cheap-looking switch-box. The starter puts its belt into motion, and the engine roars into life.

One of the robust four-cylinder unit's relative weaknesses is its clutch, and this bike's felt rather grabby as I hooked first gear and pulled away. But once into its stride the MV behaved flawlessly, surprising me by being docile at slow speed, and accelerating crisply when the ridged Tommaselli throttle was wound back from less than 2000 RPM. The motor was superbly smooth, encouraging hard riding with a slick gearbox that was a delight to use despite its unfamiliar right-boot, down-for-up change.

world championship on an MV four of very similar engine design.

The scarlet machines had dominated racing for years through John Surtees, Mike Hailwood, and Giacomo Agostini. But MV's autocratic boss, Count Domenico Agusta, had not wanted his team's achievements diluted by privateers, and for most of that time there had been no multi-cylinder roadster. When MV did belatedly introduce a roadgoing multi, in 1967, it was the ugly 600 four tourer whose softly tuned, 52 BHP shaft-drive engine gave a top speed of barely 100 mph (160 km/h).

The expensive 600 was such a flop that Count Domenico finally relented. At the Milan Show in 1969, the firm unveiled the bike that many Italian bike enthusiasts had been waiting for (although most had no chance of affording to buy). The 750 Sport had bold red, white, and blue paintwork, clip-ons, rear-sets, a humped seat, and a four-pipe exhaust system ending in slender chrome-plated megaphones.

Most magical of all was the blend of induction and exhaust roar as the tach needle flicked past 5000 RPM and the engine kicked again, bellowing out a uniquely aggressive sound that transformed the most ordinary road into a Monza straight. Top speed didn't match the factory's claimed 129 mph (225 km/h); *Cycle World* managed only 114 mph (183 km/h). But few rivals could outperform the Sport in a straight line, and its handling was very respectable, too.

Okay, so this frame wasn't as strong as the racers', and the drive shaft added 15 kg (33 lb) of weight, contributing to a substantial total of 230 kg (506 lb). But the shaft introduced very little torque reaction, and this bike's rear end was well controlled, helped by remote-reservoir Marzocchi shocks that were superior to the originals. Straight-line stability was excellent. And although the Sport felt tall and ungainly at slower speeds, its steering was precise and reasonably light.

MV Agusta 750 Sport (1973)

Engine type	Air-cooled DOHC, 8-valve transverse four
Displacement	743cc
Bore x stroke	65 x 56 mm
Compression ratio	9.5:1
Carburetion	4 x 27 mm Dell'Orto
Claimed power	65 BHP at 7900 RPM (see text)
Transmission	5-speed
Electrics	12-volt battery
Frame	Tubular steel cradle
Front suspension	35 mm telescopic Ceriani
Rear suspension	Twin Marzocchi dampers, adjustments for preload
Front brake	Two, Brembo calipers, 280 mm (11 in) discs
Rear brake	Double-action caliper, 280 mm (11 in) disc
Front tire	100/90 x 18 in
Rear tire	120/90 x 18 in
Wheelbase	1390 mm (54.7 in)
Seat height	787 mm (31 in)
Fuel capacity	24 liters (5.3 UK gal, 6.3 US gal)
Weight	230 kg (506 lb) dry

Below: Slender, chrome-plated megaphone pipes look good as well as producing a glorious and deafening sound. This bike's later Marzocchi remote-reservoir shocks help keep the rear end under control despite the weight of the drive shaft.

Sadly for MV Agusta, those attributes did not make the Sport a commercial success. Many riders would have loved to buy an MV, but very few could afford to do so—yet the exotic, hand-assembled four cost so much to build that it was not profitable despite its high price. The same was true of the more angular 750S America and 850 Monza models that followed before production ended in the late Seventies.

But more than 20 years later the Sport remains hugely valuable, and for very good reason. This superbike has it all: looks, rarity, glorious racing heritage, a wonderful sound, and most of all, fiery performance that makes it enormously fun to ride. In the case of the 750 Sport, the reality very definitely matches the reputation.

From *Bike*, SEP. 1975

"The motor is very powerful. Surprisingly, it also has great reserves of torque, and pulls happily from four thousand... It's probably the most powerful 750cc motor ever made. In a straight drag with a Kawasaki Z1, it lost only a few yards up to 100 mph [160 km/h].

As I got more used to it, so its vices emerged. It hops and lurches like the Z1 Kawa if the corner isn't completely smooth. The front forks are Cerianis, and no one ever criticized "cherries." The blame for the handling goes to the Marzocchi shocks, which were distinctly substandard.

Ideally, one would like to see a future version of the bike a little slimmer. Sixty or seventy pounds [27-32 kg] less would be enough to make it into the definitive 750. The motor doesn't need changing. Sweet, torquey, high revving and powerful, it proves that a good design goes on for years."

Kawasaki Z1-A

At an indicated 100 mph (160 mph) it's a hell of a thrill. You're crouched down in a vain attempt to escape from the wind, peering over the clocks and with arms raised to high, wide handlebars. The big engine is sucking audibly through its open-topped airbox beneath the seat, and howling louder through four chrome silencers as the mighty Z1 speeds along with the force and style that once made it the undisputed King.

Then you glance down at the steering head and realize that the handlebars don't just feel light, but that they're moving slightly yet visibly from side to side under the strain being fed into the chassis. It's not a weave, but it's not far from becoming one—and it shows the other side of the Kawasaki's personality. The motor's smoothness and easy speed could almost deceive you into thinking that this is a modern multi. But superbikes were very different when the Z1 ruled the roads.

Few riders were put off by a little high-speed instability when the Z1 arrived to rewrite the book on two-wheeled performance in 1973. This bike's 135 mph (217 km/h) top speed was over 10 mph

(16 km/h) higher than that of Honda's CB750, until then Japan's finest superbike, and the Kawasaki's standing quarter-mile time of 12.5 seconds was over a second quicker. Neither the Honda nor anything else could keep it in sight.

Yet the bike that firmly cemented Kawasaki's reputation might never have been built. In late 1968 the firm's engineers had been dismayed when, with their own plans for a four-cylinder 750 well advanced, Honda had unveiled the CB750. Rather than abandon their project, code-named "New York Steak," Kawasaki learned all they could from the opposition, enlarged their engine to 903cc, and returned four years later with the Z1.

Their efforts were rewarded, because the Z1 powerplant—with square dimensions of 66 x 66 mm, compression ratio of 8.5:1, and

Opposite: Kawasaki's 903cc, dohc eight-valve engine was the most powerful motorcycle powerplant yet produced, and also very smooth and robust. Above: Lean, attractive styling was another key reason for the Z1's huge success. Right: High handlebars did not aid comfort or handling at high speed. Lower bars were introduced for European markets with the Z1-B in 1975.

The more you know about motorcycles the more you appreciate it.

twin camshafts working eight valves—was in a class of its own. Its claimed maximum output of 82 BHP at 8500 RPM meant the Z1 was 15 BHP more powerful than the single-cam CB750, giving a lasting boost to the high-performance image that Kawasaki's fiery triples had already established.

The motor was angled slightly forward in a chassis based around a conventional twin-cradle steel frame. Front forks held a 19-inch spoked wheel, with a single disc brake. A second disc and caliper could be fitted as an extra, using lugs fitted to the right fork slider. Twin rear shocks held an 18-inch wheel with drum brake.

If the Z1's chassis specification was ordinary, then its styling was inspired. Although big and heavy, the Kawasaki looked anything but. Its slim fuel tank, small rounded side panels, rear duck-tail, and four silencers gave an eager look—rounded and gentle, yet at the same time raw and brutally powerful.

Those high handlebars and the Z1's fairly forward-set footpegs were hardly designed to help exploit the bike's all-conquering horsepower. But all these years later, the improbably relaxed riding position merely adds to the thrill as you straddle the thick seat and look out over the simple dashboard layout of twin clocks with warning lights in the center.

When the motor fires up it burbles through its four pipes with a suitably menacing sound. Otherwise, the feel is quite modern. Throttle and clutch are light, carburetion of the four 28 mm Mikunis is crisp, the five-speed gearbox slick, and the torquey motor pulls happily from 3000 RPM in top gear.

There's a little more vibration than from most modern fours, but the ride is acceptably smooth. The Z1 cruises at 80 mph (130 km/h) with just 5000 RPM showing on the tach, and with four grand still to come before the red-line. At that sort of speed the motor feels relaxed—even if the exposed riding position means that description does not apply to the rider for long.

Thoughts of comfort are forgotten, though, when at about

Right: The main difference between this Z1-A and the previous year's model was color, including that of the engine fins, which were no longer painted black. Below right: Hard cornering shows off the four exhaust pipes. Opposite, from left: The single disc brake was standard fitment until 1976—even later in some markets. A kick-starter backed up the electric starter. Original pipes were often swapped for a four-into-one system.

50 mph (80 km/h) in third gear you crack open the throttle to send the Z1 storming forward with an arm-wrenching surge of acceleration that is thrilling now and must have been mind-blowing back in the Seventies. There's still a raw urgency about the old warrior's power delivery that sends a tingle down your spine.

And the handling helps to make the ride exciting, because it's easy to see why the Kawasaki brought plenty of trade to chassis specialists such as Harris and Bakker. This immaculate, 1974-model Z1-A didn't once misbehave seriously enough to become worrying. But above 80 mph (130 km/h), its steering was light enough to make me understand why Z1 riders rarely left their bikes standard.

Fitment of a steering damper was a popular modification at the time, as was swapping the shocks for units from firms such as Koni. Slow-speed stability was helped by conservative steering geometry that meant the Z1 needed plenty of pressure on those

Kawasaki Z1-A (1974)

Engine type	Air-cooled DOHC, 8-valve transverse four
Displacement	903cc
Bore x stroke	66 x 66 mm
Compression ratio	8.5:1
Carburetion	4 x 38 mm Mikunis
Claimed power	82 BHP @ 8500 RPM
Transmission	5-speed
Electrics	12 V battery; 36/36 W headlamp
Frame	Tubular steel cradle
Front suspension	Telescopic, no adjustment
Rear suspension	Twin shock absorbers, adjustable preload
Front brake	Single 295 mm (11.6 in) disc; second disc optional extra
Rear brake	203 mm (8 in) SLS drum
Front tire	3.50 x 19 in
Rear tire	4.00 x 18 in
Wheelbase	1500 mm (59 in)
Seat height	800 mm (31.5 in)
Fuel capacity	18 liters (4 UK gal, 4.8 US gal)
Weight	246 kg (542 lb) wet

wide handlebars for rapid changes of direction. Although narrow, this bike's Metzelers gave enough grip to make grounding the centerstand easy.

Even the standard single front disc brake was fairly powerful, given a strong enough squeeze of the lever. That was just as well, because the twin-disc conversion was an expensive option at the time. (Wet-weather braking performance was appalling—with one disc or two.)

The Z1's speed made it an instant hit, and such was its lead over the opposition that Kawasaki barely had to modify their flagship for several years. This Z1-A differed from the original Z1 of 1973 in its paint scheme, alloy (instead of black) cylinder finish, and minor alterations to fork damping and carburetor jetting. The Z1-B of 1975 was cosmetically different again, and dispensed with the original model's messy drive-chain oiler.

In 1976 the second front disc became standard fitment, while smaller carbs, reshaped combustion chambers, and more restrictive pipes (to reduce emissions for the US market) reduced peak power from 82 to 81 BHP. The bike also gained a new name, becoming the Z900. But one thing didn't change. It was still the fastest, meanest motorcycle on the road.

From *Cycle World*, MAR. 1973

"The 903cc Z1 opens a whole new era for Kawasaki. It is the culmination of five years of pondering the problem of how to have your cake and eat it, too, or combining sheer performance with comfort. This Kawasaki gives away nothing in either department.

It is one of the two or three quickest road bikes in production. Yet it is luxuriously big, and politely sibilant. It goes fast in a slow way, covering ground in great bites. The Z1 is one of those shockingly understated GT bikes, the kind on which you can look down at the speedometer and discover, 'My God, I'm doing 90, I'd better slow down.'

While the Z1 is eclectic, a summation of everything we know about roadster technology, it has no parallel at present. Within the limitations of its weight, it can handle most any acceleration, turning or stopping situation that an expert rider can deal it."

BMW R90S

The speedometer shows a steady 80 mph (130 km/h) as the road ahead unwinds from a gentle curve. I'm sitting comfortably, leaning slightly forward to slightly raised handlebars, my chest and head protected from the wind by a neat half-fairing that also contains a clock and voltmeter.

The big orange fuel tank is full, giving the prospect of 200 miles (320 km) of nonstop, high-speed riding. Below the tank I can see the motor's sticking-out cylinders, their gentle rustling almost drowned by a fruity twin-cylinder exhaust note. By modern standards the mechanical and exhaust sounds are loud, but they do nothing to mar the BMW's aristocratic air.

Nor does the bike's stability, as I bank through a series of gentle curves, suspension soaking up the bumps efficiently, the tall-geared engine feeling unburstable. Never mind its generous fuel range; this bike gives the impression that it would cruise at speed and in comfort forever.

However long BMW builds flat twins, it's debatable whether there will be another to match the impact that the R90S made on its launch in 1974. The half-faired 90S, finished in a stylish

smoked color scheme (gray was the original color, with this bike's orange following as an option a year later), may have been a sportster only by BMW's traditionally restrained standards. But with a top speed of a shade over 125 mph (200 km/h), it was seriously quick by mid-Seventies standards.

The R90S was at its best traveling rapidly over long distances, but there was much more to this bike than sheer speed. Handsome, fine handling, comfortable, well equipped, and very expensive, the R90S was arguably the best all-around superbike that money could buy.

The S and its unfaired relation the R90/6, introduced at the same time, were derived from the previous R75 models. Enlarging the 745cc R75's bore from 82 to 90 mm while retaining the

Opposite: The "S" in the R90S's name stood for Sport, and the big boxer handled well enough to justify the title. Above: The addition of the headlamp fairing and unique smoked orange paint scheme transformed BMW's traditionally shaped twin into one of the most stylish bikes on the road. Right: Shaft drive meant practicality as well as performance.

70.6 mm stroke gave a capacity of exactly 900cc. BMW also took the opportunity to make numerous engine mods, including strengthening the bottom end, plus fitting a revised gearshift mechanism and new alternator.

The S model differed from the humbler 90/6 by having higher compression (9.5:1 from 9:1), and a pair of 38 mm Dell'Orto carbs with accelerator pumps in place of the basic model's 32 mm Bings. Those mods helped lift peak power output from the 90/6's 60 BHP to a claimed 67 BHP at 7000 RPM. In addition the S had a bigger gas tank, twin front brake discs instead of just one, plus,

of course, that handlebar-mounted fairing with its useful pair of dials above the normal speedo and tachometer.

BMW's high standard of finish means that this unrestored 90S's smoked paintwork still looked good after 42,000 miles (67,000 km), with just the odd minor blemish. The bike ran very well, too, after I'd reached inside the fairing to the strangely placed ignition switch, and then pressed the button to bring the boxer motor to life with its traditional side-to-side lurch. Despite its raised compression and big Dell'Ortos, the 90S was still as refined and well behaved as any BMW.

R 90 S
R 90/6 R 75/6
R 60/6

Right: Large fuel tank and the 900cc motor's efficiency combined to give a generous range between fill-ups. This boxer engine was the culmination of a line of development that stretched back to 1923 and BMW's first 500cc R32 model. Below right: Despite a modern format of twin drilled discs, the front brake lacked power and required a firm squeeze of the handlebar lever. The common Seventies fitment of a fork brace improved this bike's front-end rigidity. The fork gaiters were also added by the owner. Modern Metzeler rubber encouraged hard cornering.

The tuned S model had a little less low-rev torque than the 90/6 but was still very flexible. Its sheer performance was impressive by mid-Seventies standards, but more important was the ease with which the Bee-Em could sustain an easy high-speed cruise, thanks to its motor's lack of annoying vibration and to the way the fairing diverted most of the wind.

This bike's chassis hadn't aged quite so well, particularly its front brake, which required a mighty squeeze of the lever before the combination of tiny calipers and 260 mm (10 in) discs delivered much stopping power. Braking was never the 90S's strong point. Its original solid 200 mm (8 in) rotors had been quickly uprated after a cool reception on the bike's launch. At least the rear drum gave some welcome extra bite.

Handling and roadholding were excellent by the standards of the day, thanks to a conventional blend of steel twin-downtube

BMW R90S (1975)

Engine type	Air-cooled pushrod, 2-valve horizontally opposed twin
Displacement	900cc
Bore x stroke	90 x 70.6 mm
Compression ratio	9.5:1
Carburetion	2 x 38 mm Dell'Ortos
Claimed power	67 BHP @ 7000 RPM
Transmission	5-speed
Electrics	12 V battery; 60/55 W headlamp
Frame	Tubular steel cradle
Front suspension	Telescopic, no adjustment
Rear suspension	Twin shock absorbers, adjustable preload
Front brake	Twin 260 mm (10 in) discs
Rear brake	200 mm (8 in) SLS drum
Front tire	3.25 x 19 in
Rear tire	4.00 x 18 in
Wheelbase	1466 mm (57.7 in)
Seat height	820 mm (32.3 in)
Fuel capacity	24 liters (5.3 UK gal, 6.3 US gal)
Weight	215 kg (473 lb) wet

frame, spindly leading-axle forks, and a twin-shock rear end. This bike's forks benefit from a nonstandard brace, and its original shocks have long since been swapped for a pair of Konis. But the feel was much the same as ever: tall, stable, neutral, and fairly soft.

And if the elderly BMW felt a shade remote and unwieldy, thanks partly to its narrow 19-inch front wheel, it's worth remembering that the 90S was produced before the Japanese manufacturers had managed to make their big bikes keep all their power under control at high speed.

In this respect, as in almost every other, the R90S is a bike that has grown old very gracefully indeed. Sure, its drive shaft made itself known at times. Hard riding on bumpy surfaces would find the limits of the suspension, and under aggressive cornering on smooth roads this bike's modern Metzeler tires gave enough grip to get the engine's cylinder heads scraping.

But the R90S matched its healthy power output with a respectable fueled-up weight of 215 kg (473 lb), which helped

From *Bike*, Dec. 1975

"BMW's flagship may not be the ultimate, but it's probably the nearest anyone's got to it yet. If you've got the bread you too can have all the discerning motorcyclist needs to ride as safely and fast and comfortably as possible.

Despite its meager proportions, the superb quality glasswork keeps a surprising amount of wind off your chest and head, making 100 mph cruising perfectly practical.

You'll always find people trying to tell you horrific tales of cylinder heads ploughing the tarmac through bends, and the fearful effects of torque reaction on handling. It's crap, probably inspired by envy. The truth is the 90S is one of the best handling big bikes around.

Perhaps the worst point is the gearchange. BMWs have always been infamous for the jarring harshness of their shift, and they've done a lot to rectify it. But by comparison to most Japanese boxes, it's still far from slick."

ensure that despite its shaft drive and *gran turismo* image there were few bikes that could stay with the BMW on the road. If proof were needed of the twin's sporting potential, Reg Pridmore's 1976 US Superbike championship victory on a stock-looking boxer provided that.

Reading old road tests gives an even better indication. Among the most telling contemporary comments was the review that stated: "The R90S handles and stops almost as well as the best Italian sportster; is almost as fast as the fastest Japanese road-burner; almost as uncomplicated as the good old British twin; and almost as smooth as the best multi. When it comes to comfort, and capability for traveling at maximum speed with minimum fatigue, the R90S is second to none."

The tester concluded that while there were many bikes that did one thing superbly, the BMW was the only one that did *everything* very well. After riding the legendary R90S all these years later, that praise is easy to understand.

Ducati 860GT

I t was as the Ducati tipped into a sweeping right-hand curve that it first happened; the slight movement of the handlebars that, sure enough, continued until it was a gentle weave. Nothing serious, you understand, but I was surprised. Plenty of big bikes would have behaved in similar fashion back in the mid-Seventies, but Ducatis had a reputation for high-speed stability second to none.

In fact when looking back through some old magazine tests later, I discovered that the 860GT was criticized for precisely the same thing back in 1975. At least the cause was well known. The bike's tendency to shake its head in fast curves was traced to the high, wide handlebars, which, perhaps surprisingly, were still in place on this clean blue V-twin.

The GT's designer, noted car stylist Giorgetto Giugiaro (creator of the original VW Golf and many others), had combined the new Gran Turismo machine's striking, angular lines with handlebars that not only made sustained high-speed riding uncomfortable, but also created disruptive steering forces that even the Ducati's basically sound chassis could not completely control.

Opposite and above: High, wide handlebars and the angular styling devised by Giugiaro's Italdesign firm make the GT one of the most distinctive of Ducati V-twins. The GT name and upright riding position confirmed the bike's intended touring role. Right: Innovative fuel tank logo added to the modern feel, and would survive in modified form for more than a decade.

That did not prevent contemporary testers from giving the 860GT an enthusiastic thumbs-up, and concluding that a redesigned riding position was the only thing it needed to become a serious hit. When it was introduced, Ducati's big-bore sports-tourer was the largest-capacity bike the firm had built. And if it didn't match the glamour or sheer speed of the 900SS that would be launched shortly afterward, the GT promised plenty of performance along with considerably more comfort and practicality.

The air-cooled, 864cc V-twin motor was essentially a pair of 450 single top halves on a common crankcase, and shared the single's 86 x 75 mm dimensions. Cylinder angle was 90 degrees, drive to the single overhead camshafts was by bevel gear, and the GT used conventional valve operation. Ducati revealed that peak

DUCATI 860 GT * TECHNICAL SPECIFICATIONS

ENGINE: 90° longitudinal Vee Twin, light alloy die cast four stroke. High thermal efficiency light alloy heads with race bred bevel gear driven S.O.H.C. Bore 86 mm (3.3858 in.), stroke 74.4 mm. (2.93 in.), total displacement 864 cc (52.5 cu. in.). Compression ratio 9.2:1. Carburation by two Dell'Orto PHF 32 pumper carbs.
TRANSMISSION: primary by helical gear. Oilbath clutch, 5 speed gearbox. Final trasm.by chain.
ELECTRICAL EQUIPMENT: 12Volt - 12Ah battery, 220 Watt alternator with electronic rectifier and regulator. **ELECTRONIC IGNITION** (picture 1). Electric starter optional in combination with 32 Ah battery.
FRAME: double loop, open cradle Exclusive ipoture 1) race proven chain adjuster by eccentric swingarm mount. Wheelbase 58.5 in. Race type suspension front and rear. Deep cushion seat and GT handlebar.
BRAKES: front single 11 in. hydraulically operated disc. Rear: 7.82 in drum brake. Double front disc on request.
TIRES: front 3.50/18 - rear: 4.25/18.
WEIGHT: 445 lbs. dry.
FUEL CONSUMPTION: 52 M.p. Imp. Gal.

BERLINER MOTOR CORP.

Hasbrouck Heights, New Jersey 07604 Sole U.S. Distributor

The above specifications are subject to modification without notice.

power was produced at 6900 RPM. No figure was given for the output, which would have been just under 70 BHP at the crankshaft.

Beneath its striking blue bodywork, the Ducati's chassis was a typical Bolognese blend of tubular steel frame and firm Italian-made suspension, with Ceriani forks and Marzocchi shocks. This bike was unrestored and standard apart from its instruments and seat, which were from the following year's 860GTS.

The later seat was slightly thinner, to reduce the GT's seat height. Despite that, the Ducati felt quite tall when I climbed aboard. I quickly became conscious not just of the pulled back bars, but also of the rather forward-set footrests. The right footpeg made itself felt almost immediately, too, because as the GT had no electric starter (one had been available as an optional extra) I had to kick-start it—and the footrest was perfectly placed to come into contact with my shin.

The pain was forgotten when the big V-twin burst into life with a delightful rustling and rumbling, and proceeded to show just why it was such a superb device for a sports-tourer. Thanks partly to its low state of tune, the engine was very responsive through the midrange, sending the bike trundling rapidly for-

ward every time the throttle was tweaked to open the 32 mm Dell'Orto carbs.

Like modern big Dukes, the V-twin was snatchy below about 3000 RPM, but smoothed out from then on. Vibration wasn't a problem even up near the 7000 RPM red-line, although the engine felt best between 3500 RPM and about six grand. Generally it was more satisfying to short-shift through the five-speed box, which was so efficient that I forgave the neutral light's traditional hopelessness.

On a straight road the Ducati rumbled pretty rapidly up to an indicated 90 mph (145 km/h). Although it began to feel slightly unsteady by that speed, it would have gone on to a top speed of just over 110 mph (176 km/h). Those high bars meant you'd have to be strong-necked to hold high speeds for long, however, and even my steady 80 mph (130 km/h) cruising speed became tiring before long.

That Ducati's tendency to weave at high speed might have tarnished its reputation slightly but it was never worrying, and the bike made up for it with its handling the rest of the time. The GT's chassis rigidity and high-quality suspension gave cornering power that few bikes could approach in 1975.

Only the inappropriate and hard-compound Chen Shin tires prevented me from getting carried away and wearing away the footpegs in the corners. At least I didn't have to worry about the front tire's ability to grip when I used the front brake. The Ducati's single 280 mm (11 in) Brembo disc lacked bite and gave a very wooden feel at the lever. A second disc was available as an extra and would have been well worth having.

Ducati did at least prove that they were willing to listen to criticism, as the following year the 860GTS was launched with not just a second front disc as standard, but flatter handlebars and an electric starter, too. In many respects the GTS was basically the Gran Turismo machine that the GT should have been all along.

The later model's high-speed stability was excellent (confirming that the original model's problem was simply due to the

bars); it was well braked and started effortlessly. Being a Ducati, of course, it still had a few annoying faults, particularly the corrosion-prone paint finish and the switchgear that made it all too easy to plunge yourself into darkness when trying to operate the headlight's dipswitch.

Back in the Seventies, Ducati enthusiasts were prepared to put up with that and the high prices because the basic package was generally so sound. And that went for the original 860GT too, even if that high and wide riding position meant the bike didn't quite live up to its high-speed, long-distance potential. The original GT wasn't perfect, but as Ducati's first big sports-tourer, its place in the history books is assured.

Ducati 860GT (1975)

Engine type	Air-cooled SOHC, 2-valve 90-degree V-twin
Displacement	864cc
Bore x stroke	86 x 74.4 mm
Compression ratio	9.5:1
Carburetion	2 x 32 mm Dell'Ortos
Claimed power	Approx 70hp @ 6900 RPM
Transmission	5-speed
Electrics	12 V battery; 60/55 W headlamp
Frame	Tubular steel
Front suspension	Ceriani telescopic, no adjustment
Rear suspension	Twin Marzocchi shock absorbers, adjustable preload
Front brake	Single 280 mm (11 in) disc, second disc optional extra
Rear brake	203 mm (8 in) SLS drum
Front tire	100/90 x 18 in
Rear tire	120/90 x 18 in
Wheelbase	1511 mm (59.5 in)
Seat height	825 mm (32.5 in)
Fuel capacity	17 liters (3.7 UK gal, 4.5 US gal)
Weight	229 kg (504 lb) wet

Below: This bike's clocks, like its seat, are from the later 860GTS model whose lower handlebars gave a sportier riding position. The high-barred GT was prone to weave at speed despite its friction steering damper, whose adjuster knob is visible above the steering head. Bottom: Provided its rider wasn't in a hurry, the GT was a pleasant bike to ride.

From *Motorcyclist*, SEP. 1975

"The first look this writer had at the new 860 Ducati quite frankly turned him off. And studying the 860GT brought mixed reactions from the *Motorcyclist* staff. A couple like the approach by the machine's stylist, Mr. Guigiaro, and many current Italian automobiles are following the same design ideas. Those of us who were weaned on motorcycles that followed another design philosophy are chagrined beyond words.

(But) the 860GT was designed primarily as a touring machine. Beginning at the top (and front) of the engine we find that the valve adjustment is now accomplished via conventional adjusting screws and jam-nuts instead of valve stem caps of varying thickness as before. This makes valve clearance adjustment much simpler, but the valves don't seem to stay in adjustment quite as long.

Summing up, it should be pointed out that the Ducati is still a very singular type of motorcycle. All ball and roller bearings, expensive bevel gears and an extremely smooth powerplant, due in part to the fact that a 90-degree V-twin is easy to balance (the primary mechanical balance) and the firing impulses are such that they tend to relax rather than excite the rider…something akin to riding a cantering horse. The Ducati 860GT is an Italian answer to the GT concept as augmented (stifled?) by U.S. government safety and noise regulation, but is a thoroughly enjoyable touring mount with true racing heritage."

Benelli 750 Sei

The bright red Benelli purred down the busy main road with a smoothness that few modern bikes could match. Wind tugged at my shoulders and almost drowned out the exhaust note, but the bike remained utterly untroubled. Its mirrors were totally clear, and barely a buzz could be felt through the handlebars, footrests, or seat. If I looked down I could see the cam cover jutting out on each side of the fuel tank, but otherwise the Benelli's motor hardly made an impression at all.

That smoothness and sophistication was the six's great strength when it was launched in 1975—and arguably its biggest weakness too. The Sei was the world's only six-cylinder roadster at the time, and very stylish it was. But despite its unique powerplant, emphasized by a line of three shiny tailpipes on each side, the Benelli never made much of an impact.

The Sei was intended to be the flagship that would lead Benelli—an old family firm with a rich racing history—toward new glory under the control of Alejandro de Tomaso. The Argentinean car baron took over Benelli, by now struggling due to lack of

funds for either production or racing, in the early Seventies, and announced development of a six-cylinder superbike shortly afterwards. Those who doubted it would ever happen were proved wrong when the Sei appeared, its engine layout owing much to Honda's four-cylinder CB500.

Benelli's engineering expertise had been demonstrated as recently as 1969, when Kel Carruthers had won the 250cc world championship on a 64 BHP four. But there was no denying the similarities between the Honda and Benelli engines. Each used an SOHC layout with central cam chain, and they shared dimensions of 56 x 50.6 mm, which in the Italian bike's case gave a capacity of 748cc.

The Benelli motor incorporated some differences, notably the alternator, which sat not at the end of the crankshaft but behind the cylinders. That allowed the six-cylinder motor's crankcases to

Opposite: The Sei's modest engine output and barn-door aerodynamics limited its straight-line performance, but for an unfaired machine it was comfortable at speed. Above: Styling was pleasant rather than dramatic, and lacked the impact that a six-cylinder super-bike might have had. Right: At least the Benelli's six-pipe exhaust system emphasized the engine's unique layout.

Benelli 750 Sei (1975)

Engine type	Air-cooled SOHC, 12-valve transverse six
Displacement	748cc
Bore x stroke	56 x 50.6 mm
Compression ratio	9.8:1
Carburetion	3 x 24 mm Dell'Orto
Claimed power	71 BHP @ 8500 RPM
Transmission	5-speed
Electrics	12 V battery; 45/40 W headlamp
Frame	Tubular steel twin cradle
Front suspension	Marzocchi telescopic, no adjustment
Rear suspension	Twin Sebac shock absorbers, adjustable preload
Front brake	Twin 300 mm (11.8 in) Brembo discs
Rear brake	200 mm (7.9 in) SLS drum
Front tire	3.50 x 18 in
Rear tire	4.10 x 18 in
Wheelbase	1448 mm (57 in)
Seat height	838 mm (33 in)
Fuel capacity	23 liters (5 UK gal, 6 US gal)
Weight	220 kg (484 lb) dry

Below: The similarity of this engine to Honda's 500-four unit is no coincidence. The Sei's cylinder dimensions and many other technical features were identical. Circular cover on left is for alternator. Opposite, from left: Single overhead camshaft layout and three rather than six Dell'Ortos contributed to the 748cc engine's soft state of tune. For a six, the Benelli engine was very narrow. Twin-downtube frame was impressively strong.

be only 25 mm wider than those of Honda's four. And the Sei's narrow feel was also aided by its use of only three Dell'Orto carburetors, the outer two of which were tucked neatly beneath the fuel tank.

The engine produced a respectable maximum of 71 BHP at 8500 RPM, and sat in a chassis that worked much better than most contemporaries. The twin-cradle frame held Marzocchi forks, plus shocks either from the same firm or Sebac. Either way, the shocks were fitted with neat chromed preload–adjusting handles. Twin 300 mm (11.8 in) front Brembo discs and calipers were backed up by a drum rear brake; wheels were 18 inches in diameter.

Despite all those exhaust pipes the Sei looked a little ordinary, and was designed more as an all-rounder than a sportbike—emphasized by this 1975-model bike's official Benelli rear carrier. Settling into the thin but quite high seat for the first time, I was initially aware of my feet disappearing beneath the big lump of engine jutting out down below. Footrests were set well forward, but the trio of carbs allowed plenty of knee room.

Hitting the starter button sent those six cylinders burbling into life, and the Benelli pulled efficiently away, the motor's excellent low-rev response making for easy town riding. Despite weighing

220 kg (484 lb) dry, much of it high up, the Sei felt very well balanced, its wide bars and generous steering lock allowing easy low-speed maneuvering. The exhaust note was wonderful, too, a deep, rich, and very distinctive sound that encouraged me to play tunes by short-shifting through the slick five-speed gearbox.

There was no need for frequent gear changing to maintain a rapid pace, because simply winding back the throttle sent the Benelli shooting forward. The motor was impressively tractable, stretching my arms as it produced useful torque everywhere above 2000 RPM in top gear. That broad powerband allowed effortless overtaking, and combined with the motor's smoothness to make the Benelli one of the best bikes of its day for sustained high-speed travel.

Good handling was an important part of the Benelli's attraction, too. Suspension at both ends was firm, more typical of an Italian sportster than a high-barred roadster. In combination with the reasonably rigid frame, that suspension helped give unshakable stability in a straight line. And although this Sei began a gentle weave through 90 mph (145 km/h) curves, it never threatened to get worse.

Slower-speed cornering performance was good for a big bike, too, aided by the wide bars that gave neutral and fairly light steering. Ground clearance was rated good at the time, although it was easy to get the centerstand digging into the road on left-handers. When I found myself approaching a corner too fast, the big twin

Brembos didn't let me down.

But if the Sei was impressively smooth and responsive, there's no escaping the fact that it wasn't particularly fast. Duly impressed by the Sei's relaxed touring ability, I decided to stretch its legs a little more. Treading down into fourth at about 70 mph (115 km/h), I wound open the throttle again and crouched down behind the clocks as the Benelli surged forward.

Throttle response was instantaneous, but the acceleration was hardly dramatic, and petered out above 100 mph (160 km/h) as, back in top gear, the broad-fronted Sei battled into a slight headwind. Given enough room and still conditions, the Benelli would have reached a top speed of about 115 mph (185 km/h). But that was no match for Kawasaki's Z900 or the sportier Italian opposition. The softly tuned Sei simply didn't have the top-end horsepower or outright speed that its exotic breeding and engine layout suggested it should.

Despite those six pots, the Sei lacked the charisma of rival V-twins or triples, too, so maybe it was no surprise that the bike never sold as well as Benelli had hoped, especially as its price was high. Nevertheless the Sei remained in production with few changes until the end of the decade, when its engine was enlarged to produce the 900 Sei. But the bigger six was no more successful, and Benelli's first bid for superbike glory came to an end.

From *Bike*, Sep. 1975

"The engine's most obvious quality is its smoothness, of course. No, I did not ride at one hundred em-pee-aitch with a Martini cocktail balanced on the tank, but one couldn't fail to be impressed by the absence of vibration and its unwholesome bed-partner, fatigue.

So the Benelli is a docile, well-mannered town bike if that's what you want it to be, but a curious transformation takes place when you hit the open road and feel like getting a little weird. Yank open the three 24mm Dell'Ortos in fourth or fifth gear and you use up a week's supply of adrenalin in about two seconds flat... the Benelli Sei hauls ass, yessir.

And don't think I'm talking merely about straight-line performance. The Benelli handles almost unbelievably well considering its dimensions, and after acclimatizing myself with the machine I found I was pushing it round familiar corners a full 10–15 miles an hour quicker than I normally traverse them on my 650 Yam. I, as you've probably gathered from my thinly disguised enthusiasm, was distinctly impressed."

Triumph T160 Trident

Sometimes everything just falls into place. The sun was shining, the Trident was running perfectly, and I was slightly late taking it back to its owner—the perfect excuse for a last, fast ride. When a gap appeared in the traffic, I glanced over my shoulder, flicked down a gear, and accelerated into the outside lane.

This was the final opportunity for the big Triumph to show its class, and it did not disappoint. With the throttle wound back the Trident pulled hard, its engine feeling stronger and stronger as the revs rose. I changed into top gear at an indicated 100 mph (160 km/h) and the tach needle dropped back to 6000 RPM, the bike still accelerating gently as I crouched over the broad tank.

When I backed off for a series of curves, the Triumph remained effortlessly stable, banking to left and right with confidence-inspiring solidity. On the following straight it held an indicated 90 mph (145 km/h) with ease, exhaust note lost to the wind, plenty of power in hand, the unfaired machine's narrow, almost flat handlebars giving a good riding position for high-speed cruising.

This was genuine superbike performance from the machine

that, until the arrival of the modern Hinckley-built Triumphs, represented the pinnacle of mass-produced British motorcycling. The T160 was launched in 1975 in a desperate attempt to make the Trident model a success, following disappointing sales of the original T150 version, which had seemed dated when introduced to compete with Honda's CB750 six years earlier.

The revamped Trident could hardly have come at a more difficult time for Norton Villiers Triumph, the struggling group that owned the BSA and Norton marques, as well as Triumph. In 1974, NVT had recorded a loss of several million pounds. In the same year, the workers at Triumph's Meriden factory had begun a sit-in to protest about threatened mass job cuts.

In those circumstances the T160, which was built not at

Opposite: The T160's slim fuel tank and angled-forward engine gave a much sportier look than that of the original T150 Trident. Above: Styling still had a distinct Triumph feel, but this triple was considerably more powerful and sophisticated than the traditional twins. Right: Engine updates included an electric starter plus a crossover shaft to give a left-foot gearchange.

Meriden but at the BSA factory in Small Heath, Birmingham, was a surprisingly good bike. Arguably its most important feature was its much improved styling, which replaced the T150's angular fuel tank with a wide, rounded tank, finished in red with white flashes or alternatively white with yellow on the slightly smaller export version. Either way, this was one handsome motorbike.

The air-cooled, 740cc pushrod engine was basically that of the T150 triple that had been launched in 1969, incorporating a number of modifications, including, at last, an electric starter. Other mods included improved oil circulation and a left-foot gearchange (the triple's gearbox had been uprated from four- to five-speed two years earlier). Peak output was an unchanged 58 BHP at 7250 RPM.

Unlike the vertical T150 motor but like that of BSA's similar Rocket 3, the T160's engine was angled forward in a new steel frame, the layout of which owed much to Triumph's works production racers, including the legendary Slippery Sam. The twin lower frame tubes were raised for improved ground clearance, the engine sat higher and farther forward, and the swingarm was lengthened. The front forks were slightly steeper and shorter than before.

My first impression after climbing aboard was that the Trident felt fairly low but decidedly heavy. Weight loss was evidently not a key goal for Triumph's development team. At 228 kg (502 lb) dry, the T160 weighs 18 kg (40 lb) more than the T150, and much of that weight is carried high. The riding position is typical of a European bike of the Seventies, pulling the rider forward to

Right: The T160 arrived as the sun was setting on Triumph. The famous old logo continued to adorn the tanks of Bonneville twins into the Eighties, but Trident production was halted at the end of 1975 as Norton Villiers Triumph plunged into financial crisis. It would be another 16 years before John Bloor launched his reborn Triumph marque, with a subtly revamped logo and an all-new naked triple—called, almost inevitably, the Trident.

the narrow bars with their squidgy Triumph grips. The panel of four warning lights between speedo and tach looks unexceptional, but this is the first time the Trident had featured a neutral light.

After tickling the outer Amal carbs, I pressed the starter button and the triple motor fired up with a muted but wonderfully distinctive burbling three-cylinder sound from its pipes. Once underway, the Trident felt well balanced but undeniably heavy. On twisty country roads its combination of narrow handlebars, laid-back 28-degree steering angle (one degree steeper than the T150), and high center of gravity demanded a very forceful riding style, and didn't exactly encourage enthusiastic cornering.

Provided it was given a firm hand at the bars, though, the Trident always obeyed instructions—and the same was even more true at the higher speeds to which the triple was better suited. Suspension was excellent, soaking up most bumps and allowing

the Triumph to sweep serenely through fast curves that would have put many contemporary rivals into a wobble.

The T160's other cycle parts played their roles well, too. The pair of Dunlop TT100s showed their age by being identical in width as well as 19-inch diameter, but they gripped well enough to make good use of the Trident's much-improved ground clearance. And although the front brake was only a single 254 mm (10 in) disc, this bike's soft-compound pads, aided by the similar rear disc, slowed the heavy bike reasonably well.

If the T160's high-speed handling was impressive, it was the three-cylinder powerplant that gave the Trident its soul. The motor was torquey enough to pull crisply, if not particularly urgently, from below 30 mph (48 km/h) in top gear—but the triple responded much more enthusiastically when I kept the revs towards the 8000 RPM limit.

Revved hard, the Trident was a thrilling bike to ride, its top-end acceleration matching most bikes on the road in 1975. The 120-degree three-cylinder engine was by no means completely smooth, buzzing enough to tingle my feet through the pegs. But the Trident had a lovely, rev-happy feel that encouraged me to keep it spinning. And although its 58 BHP peak output and 125 mph (200 km/h) top speed seem moderate now, the Triumph was and still is capable of covering large distances at speed.

That was not enough to make it a big success, partly due to Triumph's mounting financial problems, which affected quality control, resulting in some unreliability. The T160's price was high, too. Despite that, about 7000 were built and sold in 1975. But by the end of that year NVT was in receivership, the Small Heath factory was about to be closed, and the Trident was finished. It was an abrupt and premature end to what was in many ways an excellent motorcycle.

Triumph T160 Trident (1975)

Engine type	Air-cooled pushrod, 6-valve triple
Displacement	740cc
Bore x stroke	67 x 70 mm
Compression ratio	9.5:1
Carburetion	3 x 27 mm Amal Concentrics
Claimed power	58 BHP @ 7250 RPM
Transmission	5-speed
Electrics	12 V battery; 45/40 W headlamp
Frame	Tubular steel
Front suspension	Telescopic, no adjustment
Rear suspension	Twin shock absorbers, adjustable preload
Front brake	Single 254 mm (10 in) disc
Rear brake	254 mm (10 in) disc
Front tire	4.10 x 19 in
Rear tire	4.10 x 19 in
Wheelbase	1473 mm (58 in)
Seat height	762 mm (30 in)
Fuel capacity	22 liters (4.8 UK gal, 5.8 US gal)
Weight	228 kg (502 lb) dry

From *Bike*, MAY 1975

"If the Trident had been like this seven years ago there wouldn't be half as many Honda fours on the road now. At last it can stand up for itself among the ranks of the world's best and most exciting heavy road-burners, without looking inadequate or inferior.

For me, riding the Trident was something of a re-discovery of the joys of British biking, and a glad realization that the sickly remnants of the country's industry is capable of presenting its products with the sort of style and finesse today's discerning market demands.

Handling has a lot to do with characteristic British feel. It's not as taut and responsive as some Italian machinery, but it gives a feeling of security and supreme confidence I've never experienced on any Japanese heavyweight... I've got a feeling the T160 is going to do a lot for the British industry's flagging reputation, here and abroad."

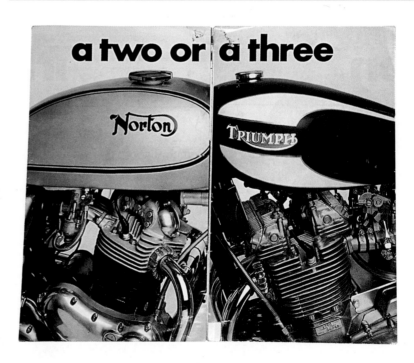

Above left: As a symbol of English industrial decline, the Trident is a lot more attractive than an old northern factory chimney. Left: Norton-type silencers reduced the triple's volume to satisfy US noise regulations, but the Trident still sounded mighty good. Above: Norton Villiers Triumph's advertising centered on "The Powerchoice" between the Commando twin and Trident triple.

Moto Guzzi 750 S3

Of all the retro-bikes produced since motorcycle manufacturers discovered the value of nostalgia, none can have been a more faithful reproduction than the handsome naked 1000S that Moto Guzzi introduced in 1990. The reason is clear when you set eyes on the 1975-model 750 S3. The bike on which the 1000S was based is a gorgeous machine, with its long and low shape, big transverse V-twin motor, and especially the sculpted fuel tank with its two broad diagonal stripes.

Back in the mid-Seventies, that distinctive naked silhouette belonged to a sports bike, not a piece of two-wheeled nostalgia. The S3 didn't merely look good, it also had the performance to match: stable handling, excellent braking, and an ability to cover long distances at a speed that few other mid-Seventies machines could match.

The S3 owed its name to just one aspect of its chassis: the triple-disc linked braking system that was introduced on this bike and also the 850 T3 tourer. The S3 was a development of the similarly styled 750 S, which had twin front discs and a drum rear—and

which itself was developed from Guzzi's first sporting V-twin, the drum-braked V7 Sport.

Even without the linked system, that trio of big 300 mm (11.8 in) discs and their Brembo calipers would have been a noteworthy feature in 1975, when rivals as glamorous and expensive as BMW's R90S flagship made do with a rear drum. But more than any one particular feature, it's the Guzzi's combination of parts—from the clip-on bars via the big lump of engine all the way to the black, shark's-gill tailpipes—that makes this bike so stylish and purposeful.

The S3's pushrod-operated 90-degree V-twin engine was heavily based on that of the V7 Sport, sharing its bore and stroke dimensions of 82.5 x 70 mm (for a capacity of 748cc), its 9.8:1 compression ratio, and most mechanical parts. But Guzzi had made some

Opposite: The S3's 748cc transverse V-twin engine was in a relatively soft state of tune, thanks to small 30mm Dell'Orto carbs plus a camshaft borrowed from the 850cc T3 tourer. Above: Striking striped paint scheme came from the previous year's 750S model, to which the S3 added a linked rear disc brake. Right: Optimistic speedometer was a typical Guzzi tuning ploy.

Moto Guzzi 750 S3 (1975)

Engine type	Air-cooled pushrod, 2-valve transverse V-twin
Displacement	748cc
Bore x stroke	82.5 x 70 mm
Compression ratio	9.8:1
Carburetion	2 x 30 mm Dell'Ortos
Claimed power	72 BHP @ 7000 RPM
Transmission	5-speed
Electrics	12 V battery; 45/40 W headlamp
Frame	Tubular steel cradle
Front suspension	Telescopic, no adjustment
Rear suspension	Twin shock absorbers, adjustable preload
Front brake	Twin 300 mm (11.8 in) Brembo discs
Rear brake	300 mm (11.8 in) Brembo disc (linked system)
Front tire	3.25 x 18 in
Rear tire	3.50 x 18 in
Wheelbase	1492 mm (58.7 in)
Seat height	730 mm (29 in)
Fuel capacity	22 liters (4.8 UK gal, 5.8 US gal)
Weight	227 kg (500 lb) wet

Below: Clip-on handlebars, a low seat, and high footpegs combine to give an aggressive but not very comfortable riding position. Opposite, from left: Firm shocks helped hide the jacking effect of the drive shaft. Foot-operated rear brake was linked to one of the front discs. The Guzzi was stable and good fun in bends, provided gear changing was sorted out well in advance. The S3's blend of low bars, striped paintwork, and big V-twin powerplant is so stylish, it's not surprising that Guzzi copied it on the 1000S 15 years later.

changes, most notably incorporating a proper oil filter in the crankcases (the Sport made do with a mere strainer), and replacing the earlier model's helical gear camshaft drive with a cheaper chain and sprockets.

One of the Guzzi's main assets was its lack of height, which was largely due to the way in which the steel frame's main spine ran between those big sticking-out cylinders. This meant that the thinly padded seat was just 730 mm (29 in) from the ground, making the S3 manageable for shorter riders. But the high footrests and the long stretch forward across the tank to the clip-ons combine with this to make a bike that would doubtless be perfectly comfortable for a chimpanzee, but results in stretched arms and cramped knees for anyone else.

The S3 fired up with that age-old transverse V-twin lurch to the right, but it didn't have quite as much low-rev judder as the firm's bigger V-twins. The sensations it delivered were all unmistakably Guzzi, though: the shaft-drive bike's rather sudden take-off when I let out the clutch, the pressure from the tappet-covers on

my knees, and most of all the aural blend of ticking valvegear, chuffing exhaust note, and hollow induction note as the revs rose.

This bike's throttle was rather heavy, and the effort of wrenching it wide open wasn't rewarded in as dramatic a way as I'd expected. With a claimed maximum of 72 BHP at 7000 RPM, the S3 was powerful, on paper. But perhaps the similar V7 Sport's claimed output of 52 BHP, delivered at the rear wheel rather than the crankshaft, gave a more accurate picture of the later model's performance. (Manufacturers' figures during this period were notoriously unreliable.)

What was for sure was that the S3's 747cc motor had less low and midrange torque than the larger-capacity Guzzis that followed it, and needed to be revved between 5000 RPM and the 7000 RPM yellow-line to give its best, which wasn't what I'd expected of a big Guzzi. Even then, the acceleration was not exactly dramatic. The S3's top speed when tested in 1975 was 125 mph (200 km/h), and its standing quarter an even less impressive 14.6 seconds—over a second slower than the R90S, let alone the mighty Z1.

But if the Guzzi took a fair bit of time to reach an indicated 90 mph (145 km/h), what it excelled at was holding that speed to the

horizon and beyond. The S3's smoothness combined with tall gearing to make for effortless riding. Its lack of midrange necessitated fairly frequent use of the rather slow five-speed gearbox, but the Guzzi felt reassuringly strong and lightly stressed.

The trio of big linked discs meant that the S3 could brake hard, too—it's doubtful whether any bike stopped more quickly in '75. Treading on the foot-pedal operated the rear Brembo, plus one of the front pair of discs; the handlebar lever added the second front disc, and could be ignored to allow easier throttle-blipping if you weren't trying to use every bit of the front tire's grip.

Handling was also very impressive, in a traditional Guzzi way. The S3 steered pretty slowly but was so stable that nothing would throw it off its cornering line. Suspension at both ends was firm without being excessively harsh, though the heavy shaft-drive rear end inevitably felt a bit remote. And the grip from this bike's modern 18-inch Michelin rubber showed ground clearance to be excellent.

Details such as the hard-to-use centerstand, dim warning lights, and awful switchgear lost the Guzzi marks, as did its high price. But to the average mid-Seventies motorcyclist, any complaints would have been far outweighed by the S3's glamour and performance. Even so, only a relatively small number of S3s were produced before Guzzi replaced it with the 850cc Le Mans a year later. The sleek and beautiful 750 S3 was gone, but it was not forgotten. The appearance of the 1000S, 15 years later, would provide proof of that.

From *Bike*, DEC. 1975

"Starting with the heart of the matter, the engine, let's point out that this is one of the surprisingly few motorcycles that will hold cruising speeds in the high nineties without feeling like it's going to scatter its internals over the tarmac.

But while the Guzzi is an effortless high speed cruiser, it will fall short of many people's expectations because it doesn't accelerate in the manner to which we've become accustomed in our latter-day 'superbikes'... Even when you buzz the motor above five grand the bike doesn't seem to lunge forward with the brute force of other biggies.

The motor has an odd wheezing sound that somehow fits the bike's loping style. Laying over the big tank, you aim the Guzzi into turns and it feels very predictable, very reassuring... However the Guzzi isn't the day-long full tilt land cruiser that we'd hoped for. The riding position, not the machine itself, makes that impossible."

Honda CB400F

It was a thoughtful gesture that on another day might well have saved me a big fine, or even my license. The motorcyclist riding in the opposite direction flashed his headlight repeatedly, then waved frantically at me in an obvious warning of trouble up ahead.

He need not have bothered. Sure enough, just around the next curve in the road was a policeman taking aim with a radar gun. But I didn't need to move a muscle (let alone miss a heartbeat) as I went past him, crouched down behind the Honda's clocks, throttle on the stop in top gear. The little CB400F was indicating just 70 mph (115 km/h) into a headwind, and was within the speed limit.

Once that danger was passed, dropping down a gear got the Honda's motor spinning harder and released a little extra power, edging my speed up toward 80 mph (130 km/h). And although by today's standards even that performance is feeble, the 400-four impressed me. Great looks, agile handling and a smooth motor made it easy to see why this bike is still talked of fondly, and regarded as a true superbike by many riders years after numerous bigger and faster contemporaries have been forgotten.

The Honda certainly made an impact in some countries when it was launched in 1975. This was largely due to its aggressive "European" personality at a time when many Japanese bikes were relatively soft, designed primarily for the American market. The 400F's size, styling, and sporting intent provided a welcome antidote for performance-hungry riders and earned many favorable reviews, summed-up by *Bike* magazine's cover line: "Poor Boy's Musclebike."

Soichiro Honda had described his company's earlier CB350 four as the "finest, smoothest Honda ever built," and the CB400F's engine was heavily based on the 350's eight-valve unit. Bore was increased by 4 mm to give a capacity of 408cc, and the motor retained a central chain to a single overhead camshaft. Peak output

Opposite: Honda's 408cc four-cylinder engine might have produced just 37 BHP, but it was smooth, sophisticated, and powerful enough to justify the Super Sport tank logo. Above: Left side view, almost free of exhaust system, was pleasingly clean and simple. Right: Cranking into a left-hand bend highlighted the Honda's handling and gave a good view of its downpipes.

400 FOUR

Left: One of the very few changes Honda made to the four throughout its life was to mount the rear footrests to the frame, as with this later CB400F2, instead of to the swing arm. Opposite: The CB400F's four-into-one exhaust system, with its quartet of near-parallel downpipes sweeping across the front of the motor, was like nothing seen before on a production bike.

was 37 BHP at 8500 RPM, competitive with rival two-strokes.

The chassis consisted of a steel frame holding conventional forks, twin rear shocks, and 18-inch wire wheels. But if that format was unremarkable, the Honda's distinctive appearance turned plenty of heads. Flat handlebars, a slim seat, and footrests positioned rearward by Seventies standards gave a decidedly sporty riding position.

Paint finish was striking, too: either plain scarlet or navy blue for the original model (yellow and this bike's darker red were later options), with the words "Super Sport" picked out beneath the Honda logo on the tank. And the classiest touch of all was a unique four-into-one exhaust system whose downpipes swept diagonally across the front of the engine.

Sporty the 400F might have been in its day, but this bike felt relaxed and even quite roomy, giving only a slight lean forward

to the bars. A kick-start was provided, but the engine started on the button and ran with a mix of top-end mechanical rattle and a deep, deceptively powerful-sounding exhaust note.

This bike's clutch was heavy, but apart from that the little Honda was great around town: maneuverable, quick, and comfortable. At low speeds it pulled obediently through the midrange, staying smooth apart from a slight tingle at about 5000 RPM. But there was a distinct power step at 6000 RPM, and in the higher gears the Honda took an age to accelerate unless kept between 8000 RPM and the ten-grand red-line.

That peakiness necessitated plenty of flicking up and down through the six-speed gearbox. On a twisty road this wasn't a problem, but over longer distances the lack of torque got a bit tiresome. On a flat road with a small rider tucked down on the tank, the 400F was good for just over 100 mph (160 km/h). But on a blustery day, with my jacket catching every gust of wind, the Honda had little speed left above 75 mph (120 km/h), and refused to hold even that figure in top gear.

Maintaining a respectable cruising pace therefore meant staying mostly in fifth, and my progress was not enhanced by rather vague handling. At speed the Honda's suspension felt harsh, and the handlebars twitched from time to time as the wind made me hang on tight and put extra force through the handlebars.

Stability at slower speeds was fine, and even all these years later it was easy to see why the 400F gained such a good reputation for handling. At 178 kg (392 lb) wet it was respectably light. Equally important, the 400's frame was rigid, and its suspension fairly firm and well damped. This bike's modern tires helped by providing plenty of cornering grip.

Braking from the single front disc was reasonably powerful, given a firm squeeze of the lever. For hard stopping, the Honda

benefited from use of the rear drum—and that would doubtless have been even more true in the rain, as the disc had a reputation for wet-weather delay. That was one of very few criticisms of the 400F in its day, though, and details such as switches, instruments, and stands were to Honda's normal high standard.

Most people who rode the four loved it, and all these years later—as I accelerated out of a corner with the bike stable, the engine revving hard, and the exhaust note singing—it was easy to see why. This bike has a knack for making you feel good, and never mind the fact that it wasn't particularly fast even in 1975. It was quick enough for many riders, plus its reliability, fuel economy, and competitive price meant that you didn't have to be rich to own one.

Those attributes made the 400F a hit in Europe, though less so in the States, where capacity counts. The four survived almost

Honda CB400F (1975)

Engine type	Air-cooled SOHC, 8-valve transverse four
Displacement	408cc
Bore x stroke	51 x 50 mm
Compression ratio	9.4:1
Carburetion	4 x 20 mm Keihins
Claimed power	37 BHP @ 8500 RPM
Transmission	6-speed
Electrics	12 V battery; 50/35 W headlamp; 156W generator
Frame	Tubular steel cradle
Front suspension	Telescopic, no adjustment
Rear suspension	Twin shock absorbers, adjustable preload
Front brake	Single 267 mm (10.5 in) disc
Rear brake	160 mm (6.3 in) SLS drum
Front tire	3.00 x 18 in
Rear tire	3.50 x 18 in
Wheelbase	1359 mm (53.5 in)
Seat height	787 mm (31 in)
Fuel capacity	14 liters (3.1 UK gal, 3.7 US gal)
Weight	178 kg (392 lb) wet

HONDA

More sense, more style.

Below: Peak power arrived at 8500rpm, and the little Honda four needed revving hard to give its best. Top speed in ideal conditions was just over 100mph (160km/h), but a headwind reduced this considerably even when the bike was fitted with European market flat handlebars.

From *Bike*, JUN. 1975

"Although the rev-counter isn't red-lined until the dizzy 10,000 RPM mark, there's plenty of power from way down the scale, which makes urban travel more manageable than on most multi-cylinder bikes.

It's a very compact motorcycle, both in styling and handling, so you have no trouble dropping it into corners or making rapid line changes in S-bend sections. What helps considerably is that for once here's a Japanese bike that's got its rear suspension properly sorted. It neither wallows in customary Japanese fashion, nor does it rattle your spine like many an Italian bike.

If you've ever wanted one of the big multis but could never quite afford it, consider the CB400. What Honda have done is to get some of the feel and style of musclebike riding into a very competitively priced package that'll hold its own in any gathering of biking cognoscenti."

unchanged for several years, competing successfully for sales against bigger machines, as well as two-stroke middleweights from Yamaha, Kawasaki, and Suzuki. This bike is actually a later CB400F2 model, but differed from the original only in its color, the location of the fuel tank cap, and in having its pillion footrests mounted on solid subframe loops, rather than on the swingarm as before.

Ironically it was competition from Honda itself that did most to kill off the four. The twin-cylinder CB400T, launched in 1977, was slightly faster and more powerful, handled just as well, was more comfortable, and cost slightly less. It also lacked the style, character, and charm of the four—but the CB400F's days as the ultimate four-stoke middleweight were numbered.

Ducati 900SS

The moment I saw it, I knew the 900SS had to be mine. The silver-and-blue Ducati stood in the window of my local motorcycle dealership, overshadowing every other machine in the showroom with its aggressive styling and supremely purposeful engineering. To this teenage Italian-bike fanatic with his nose pressed up against the glass, the Super Sport was quite simply the most desirable motorcycle in the world.

The year was 1979, so the early-model Ducati would have been several years old, but its condition was immaculate. This bike's price was well below that required for a new 900SS, and I had an old Triumph to trade in, plus a drawer full of cash from nine months of laboring work since leaving school. I quickly reached a deal with the salesman, agreeing to pay the balance over the months to come.

Sadly, I never did buy that Ducati. The shop wouldn't sell me the bike without a signature to confirm that my parents would take over the monthly payments if necessary—and my dad refused, point blank. He was right, of course. I was due to start a college course in six months' time, and you don't run a superbike

on a student grant and holiday jobs (even if you are prepared to forgo food, drink, and other nonessentials).

The whole idea was crazy—but then the Ducati affected people like that in the Seventies. Some rival superbikes had more power; and many provided exciting performance with far greater practicality. But for sheer sporting speed and style, the 900SS got my vote every time.

The original 900 Super Sport owed much to Ducati's racing exploits—notably the 1972 Imola 200, in which factory pilots Paul Smart and Bruno Spaggiari scored a famous one-two against a strong lineup, including Agostini on a 750cc MV Agusta.

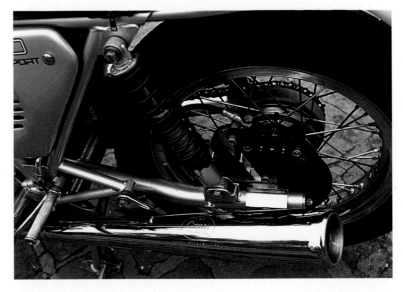

Opposite: Half fairing and clip-on handlebars gave the slender 900SS an aerodynamic edge over most rivals in the mid-Seventies. Above: The 900's supremely racy profile was almost identical to that of the even more exotic 750SS that had begun Ducati's Super Sport line in 1974. Right: Booming Contis and stiff Marzocchis were a vital part of the 900SS experience.

The following year Ducati produced a small batch of 25 road-legal production racers, closely based on the winning bike and called the Imola Replica.

Such was the demand that Ducati built more of the 750SS, as the model became known. Like the first replicas, each was fitted with a fiberglass fuel tank and neat half fairing. The engine was the 748cc V-twin engine from Ducati's 750 Sport, uprated with desmodromic valve operation, high-compression forged pistons, and polished engine internals. A total of about 200 were built, several of which were raced successfully during 1974.

For 1975 Ducati produced the 900SS by replacing the smaller engine with a V-twin unit based on that of the 860GT. This used a bigger, 86 mm bore with the original 74.4 mm stroke, giving 864cc. Fabio Taglioni's V-twin format had already become a Ducati trademark: air-cooled cylinders at 90 degrees, bevel drive to single overhead camshafts. Like the 750SS, the new bike featured desmo valvegear, polished conrods, 40 mm Dell'Orto carbs, and free-breathing Conti pipes. Peak output was 79 BHP at 7000 RPM at the crankshaft, 68 BHP at the rear wheel.

This 1975-model 900SS is almost certainly from Ducati's first-ever batch, as it was built using chassis parts left over when production switched from the 750SS. The whole bike is starkly functional, from the clip-on bars, racy half fairing, and twin drilled Brembo discs at the front to the rear-set footrests and the storage

area in the hump of its thinly padded single seat. There's no electric starter, no indicators, nothing that isn't needed for pure performance.

Elderly Super Sports can be fiendishly hard to start, but this bike responded to a firm kick by firing up every time, with a deep and utterly gorgeous bark through the open Contis. This bike emphatically was not built for slow-speed riding, as the briefest of journeys through town confirmed. Its riding position stretches you out over the long tank, with feet high though not particularly cramped. The front end absorbed bumps reasonably well, but the firmly suspended rear clanked over potholes that I'd barely have noticed on many bikes.

A tall first gear didn't help in town, either, although at least the engine was docile even at low speeds, feeling smooth and delightfully torquey as it slurped loudly through the big unfiltered Dell'Ortos. And when I reached the open road, the Ducati immediately came into its own. Given a simple twist of the throttle, it surged toward the horizon, picking up speed smoothly and with a seamless power delivery, its exhaust note hardening to a crescendo as the revs rose toward the 7000 RPM red-zone.

In '75 the 900SS came with a right-foot gearchange, and a down-for-up pattern. Despite slight wear in the lever, the change

Right: The Ducati's front-end combination of Marzocchi forks, twin drilled Brembo discs, 18-inch diameter Borrani wheel rims, and Pirelli Phantom rubber was as good as it got in 1975. Below right: Few contemporary rivals came close to matching either the 900SS's high-speed stability or its relaxed feel when traveling very fast indeed. Combine those attributes with its style, sound, and V-twin character, and it's easy to see why some riders were willing to pay its high price and put up with its demanding nature.

was pretty good (later left-foot conversions were regarded as less precise, due to the complicated linkage). The Ducati could be flicked easily through its five-speed box given a helping blip of the throttle with each downchange, though its glorious midrange delivery meant minimal gearchanging was required.

In a straight line the Ducati was capable of about 135 mph (215 km/h) in standard trim; good enough to see off almost all opposition in '75. More important for road use, it cruised at 100 mph (160 km/h) with a nonchalant, long-legged ease. The fairing was effective for fast riding, provided I crouched down behind the screen. It contributed to the Ducati's legendary stability, too.

Through a couple of 90 mph (145 km/h) curves the SS handlebars began to feel a bit vague, but the rest of the time the bike simply went just where it was pointed. Its combination of light

Ducati 900SS (1975)

Engine type	Air-cooled SOHC, desmodromic 2-valve 90-degree V-twin
Displacement	864cc
Bore x stroke	86 x 74.4 mm
Compression ratio	9.5:1
Carburetion	2 x 40 mm Dell'Orto
Claimed power	79 BHP @ 7000 RPM
Transmission	5-speed
Electrics	12 V battery; 60/50 W headlamp
Frame	Tubular steel
Front suspension	Marzocchi telescopic, no adjustment
Rear suspension	Twin Marzocchi shock absorbers, adjustable preload
Front brake	2 x 280 mm (11 in) Brembo discs
Rear brake	229 mm (9 in) Brembo disc
Front tire	3.50 x 18 in
Rear tire	120/90 x 18 in
Wheelbase	1500 mm (59in)
Seat height	770 mm (30.3 in)
Fuel capacity	18 liters (4 UK gal, 4.7 US gal)
Weight	188 kg (414 lb) dry

Below: There was no room for a passenger on this most spartan of superbikes, which had no indicators or electric starter. Ducati offered a dual-seat in some markets from 1978, and fitted an electric starter in the early Eighties. By then the SS had been detuned with smaller carbs and a more restrictive exhaust, and had lost much of the original's raw appeal.

weight, efficient steel-tube frame, long-wheelbase geometry, and Marzocchi suspension parts at front and rear made for fairly slow steering and a wonderfully unshakeable cornering feel, even when the stiff rear shocks kicked over bumps. The Brembo brakes were powerful, and the narrow Pirelli Phantoms gripped well enough to make good use of the Ducati's abundant ground clearance.

Before riding the Ducati, I'd worried that even this superb example would not live up to expectations; that I'd finally have to admit that the original 900SS was nothing like as good as I'd believed all those years ago. On the contrary, I came away from this test buzzing from the Ducati's brilliance and with my adulation reinforced. I'll own one some day, no question. It's only a matter of time.

From *Bike*, Nov. 1978

"The advantage of the desmo valve gear is at high RPM, but the real joy of riding the 900SS is the massive torque that floods in from 2000 RPM, giving the bike a most un-racer-like tractability and the rider a most-racer-like ability.

It's difficult to be caught in the wrong gear on the 900SS, which goes a long way to explaining its rapidity through the twisty bits. And yet when you come to the straights and zap open the Tommaselli quick action throttle, the Conti exhausts take on a hard edged *blat* that seems to hang around your ears, and the tacho needle spins very quickly to the red zone.

The Ducati 900SS is possibly the purest form of motorcycling there is, a kind of Nirvana of the thrills and sensations that make it all worthwhile. But it wouldn't suit everyone, or even most bikers, so be careful before committing yourself. Street Racing For Real? Well, maybe."

Laverda 750 SFC

The tach needle rose toward 8000 RPM, and then fell as I trod up through the gearbox with the heel of my right boot on the unusual rocking lever. Crouching low over the long orange fuel tank, I peered through the screen as the road unwound and the Laverda surged forward with a distinctive exhaust note and a drumming of parallel-twin vibration through its thin seat.

I didn't bother looking for the speedometer—there wasn't one in the cockpit of this most single-minded of sport machines. As the midday sun beat down on my black leathers, it wasn't hard to imagine that I was racing at Montjuic Park in Barcelona in the early Seventies, hammering Laverda's 750 SFC around the twisty street circuit with a few hours to go to the end of the famous 24-hour race.

When you ride a bike as purposeful and as full of character as the SFC on good roads, it's easy to see why the bike made such an impact. The twin's lean, handsome styling perfectly complements the personality revealed by its clip-ons and rear-sets, and its racy bodywork—finished in the vivid orange that Laverda used

because it made the factory endurance racers easier to spot as they thundered past the pits in the long night of a 24-hour marathon.

The 750 SFC was a true racebike on the road. It was launched in 1971 as an endurance-racing version of Laverda's SF series of 750cc parallel twins, the C of its name standing for Competizione. A tuned engine, strengthened with revised bearings and larger oil pump, sat in a revised frame that held a racy half fairing and seat unit.

Opposite: The SFC's footrests were much higher and farther back than on Laverda's SF roadsters. Left-foot rear-brake operation was common on Italian bikes in the mid-Seventies, and in this case is by disc rather than drum. Above: In layout, specification, and even paint finish, the SFC was a racer on the road. Right: Its handling was a match for anything in 1975.

the bike came both with twin roadgoing silencers and a two-into-one race pipe. The two machines pictured show both systems. The twin-pipe SFC is an unrestored 1975 model, while the other is a replica, built by Palmelli, a firm of English Laverda specialists using reconditioned and specially manufactured parts.

Visually the replica is identical to a late-model SFC. But while this bike's 744cc SOHC engine and some cycle parts are original, its bodywork and frame are new. The motor is also detuned with a lower 9:1 compression ratio, and it has a roadster five-speed gearbox in place of the original close-ratio unit. The crankshaft had been converted to a 90-degree firing arrangement, instead of the normal 360 degrees, for smoother running.

Ergonomics are uncompromising, with a long reach forward to the bars and not much distance between the seat and the high footpegs. The replica, producing slightly less power than the original's 75 BHP at the crank, fired up with a softer bark than I'd expected from that two-into-one pipe. Unlike a normal SFC, it idled happily and pulled crisply, even with as little as 2500 RPM showing on the tachometer.

An SFC with race pipes was reckoned to be good for 130 mph. This bike felt mighty fast as it flashed down a narrow country road, its rider concentrating hard to master the unfamiliar heel-and-toe gearchange. The parallel twin put out a fair amount of vibration, but it wasn't a problem except between 3500 and 4500 RPM, when the motor buzzed uncomfortably through the seat.

By Seventies standards the Laverda had a superb chassis. Its rigid frame, light weight, and taut suspension kept the twin stable when most rivals would have lost their cool. Inevitably the aging SFC with its 18-inch diameter wheels felt a bit cumbersome by modern standards, but the steering was very neutral.

The rebuilt Ceriani forks and Koni shocks gave a firm ride in the best Italian sportster tradition, and Brembo's brake setup, although feeling a bit wooden, stopped the bike quite hard. There was

An SFC won its first race, the Barcelona 24 Hours at Montjuic Park; many others were ridden on the street, after a few minor modifications. Initially fitted with a drum front brake, the SFC was one of the fastest bikes on the road in the early Seventies. It was expensive, though, and fewer than 100 were built in each of the first three years.

In 1974 Laverda updated the SFC with triple disc brakes, thicker Ceriani forks, and subtly restyled bodywork. When new,

plenty of ground clearance, despite the provision of a center-stand, and sticky Pirelli tires made using it good fun.

I took things slightly easier on the original twin, which was in good condition although many parts were worn and tarnished and the bike hadn't been ridden for some time before my test. The motor was noisier than the more recent unit, and felt slightly rougher due largely to its original 360-degree crankshaft, but still pulled crisply.

The most noticeable difference was not its performance but the heavy feel of its clutch. In typical SFC style the motor wasn't keen on ticking over, and slow-speed running was not helped either by the way that the fairing tried to slice off my fingers when using all of the bike's less than generous steering lock.

But at least I knew how fast I was going, as the SFC headed toward a top speed of about 130 mph (210 km/h), because this bike was fitted with Jota-style instruments in place of the single tach that was all the Breganze factory supplied. Handling was pretty good, although the aging Ceriani shocks were harsher than the replica's Konis. The original model was less fun to ride, but to many SFC enthusiasts a bike's history is every bit as important as its performance.

Laverda updated the SFC again with electronic ignition and cast wheels, although the majority were wire-spoked. The last models were the fastest, especially when fitted with the optional 6C factory camshaft that gave added high-rev power and a top speed of 135 mph (217 km/h).

Only 549 examples of the SFC were built before production ended in 1976, which helps explain the sky-high prices that clean examples command. More even than most Seventies superbikes, the stylish 750 SFC promises more speed than its elderly engine can deliver. But there's still a real magic about the fiery orange twin.

Laverda 750 SFC (1975)

Engine	Air-cooled SOHC, 2-valve parallel twin
Displacement	744cc
Bore/stroke	80 x 74 mm
Compression ratio	10.5:1
Carburetion	2 x 36 mm PHB Dell'Orto carbs
Transmission	5-speed box, chain final
Power	75 BHP @ 7500 RPM
Frame	Tubular steel
Front suspension	38 mm Ceriani telescopic forks
Rear suspension	2 x Koni shock absorbers, adjustable for pre-load and rebound damping
Front brake	2 x 280 mm (11 in) Brembo discs, 2-piston calipers
Rear brake	280 mm (11 in) disc, 2-piston Brembo caliper
Front tire	110/90 x 18 in
Rear tire	120/90 x 18 in
Wheelbase	1475 mm (58 in)
Seat height	750 mm (29.5 in)
Fuel capacity	25 liters (5.5 UK gal, 6.6 US gal)
Weight	206 kg (453 lb) dry

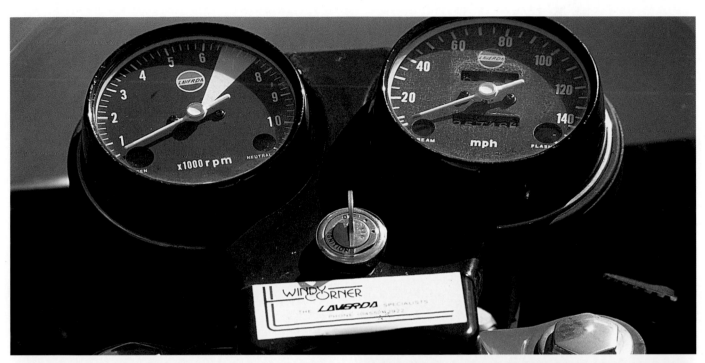

Honda GL1000 Gold Wing

Can any bike have generated such contrasting emotions as the Honda Gold Wing did on its launch in 1975? America fell in love with the Wing straight away. *Cycle* magazine devoted eight pages to a glowing review that began: "If Honda is going to sell a motorcycle for $3000, then by all that's holy it's going to be worth it." Before long US sales were booming, and the Gold Wing was on its way to becoming one of motorcycling's longest-lasting success stories.

Things were rather different on the other side of the Atlantic. *Bike*, the best-selling British monthly, followed the headline "Two Wheeled Motor Car?" by describing the GL1000 as ugly, overweight, too complicated, and boring. That lost the magazine Honda's advertising for a year. Most Europeans were more positive, but the Gold Wing's reception was decidedly mixed.

Perhaps the most surprising thing, given all that fuss, is just how ordinary the original GL1000 now seems. By modern touring standards the Honda is not so much complex and overweight as basic and underequipped. There's no fairing, top-box, passenger backrest, or panniers. No sound system or cruise control, and certainly no reverse gear, as on the Wing of today. (Not that any other mid-Seventies bikes had such features either, of course.)

Honda's development team had begun work in 1972. Their first prototype was a 1470cc flat six, code-named the AOK and similar in appearance to the final machine. But although the engine reportedly worked well, its length created problems. Instead, Honda's engineers opted for a flat-four engine whose dimensions of 72 x 61.4 mm gave a capacity of 999cc. Single overhead camshafts were driven by toothed rubber belts. Peak power was 80 BHP at 7500 RPM.

The Wing's chassis was relatively conventional, based around a tubular steel frame, though it incorporated a dummy fuel tank that contained some electrical components, a kick-start lever, and

Opposite: Honda's liquid-cooled flat-four engine was bulky and distinctive, but the size of the bike itself kept things in proportion. Above: In profile the Gold Wing looked conventional, if slightly overweight. Most GLs were soon fitted with fairings and luggage, though these accessories were not initially produced by Honda. Right: Shaft drive was a vital part of the tourer's specification.

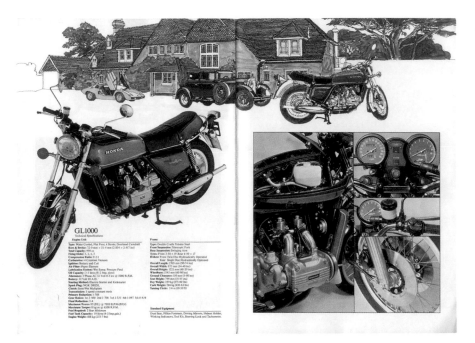

GL1000

have back in the mid-Seventies. Then, the Honda's standing quarter-mile time of just under 13 seconds meant that, with the exception of Kawasaki's Z1, it was the hardest-accelerating production bike in the world. Top speed was slightly over 120 mph (193 km/h), but the motor's long-legged cruising ability was its most impressive feature.

The Gold Wing was as smooth and effortless at 80 mph (130 km/h) as it was at half that speed, and had enough midrange power to make revving it toward the 8500 RPM red-line rarely necessary. That, combined with its light five-speed gearbox (this bike's liking for false neutrals was typical), its competent shaft drive arrangement, and a rapidly earned reputation for reliability, enabled the Wing to give the impression that it would cruise to the ends of the earth in relaxed comfort.

Unfortunately, that wasn't the case. The Honda's exposed, high-bar riding position was not suited to long distances and the seat was not very comfortable. That was less serious than it should have been, because the underseat fuel tank held only 19 liters (4.2/5 UK/US gal), enough for not much more than 100 miles (160 km) if the performance was used. In addition, the fuel gauge in the dummy tank was hopelessly pessimistic and got in the way of a tank bag.

Handling was never likely to be the Wing's forte, but although it always felt like a big bike, its low center of gravity meant that walking-pace maneuvering was easy. The wide bars made steering fairly light, despite the long wheelbase and 19-inch front wheel. You certainly couldn't call the Wing agile, but it was less of a handful than I'd expected.

Some early tests reported a high-speed weave when the Honda was shod with its original fitment Dunlops. But this bike wore more modern rubber, and both stability and grip were good. The Wing's skinny forks were fairly firm, but the rather

a small amount of storage space. Fuel lived under the seat, which helped lower the center of gravity of a bike that, at 290 kg (638 lb) with fuel, was far heavier than most others.

Modern giant tourers, including the current Gold Wing, weigh far more, so not surprisingly the naked original Wing didn't feel particularly massive. This bike was a K1 model from 1976. Apart from its paint scheme, the K1 was virtually identical to the original K0, differing only in a few added details such as helmet locks and a grease nipple on the drive shaft housing.

This GL's big motor started easily and very smoothly, breathing out very quietly through its twin exhausts and emitting very little noise from the water-jacketed cylinders in front of my shins. Controls were as light as you'd expect of a Honda, but this bike was reluctant to idle, and pulled away with a slight, carb-related low-speed hesitation that is fairly common with old GL1000s.

In every other way, though, the GL motor felt just as it must

soft shocks began to feel vague and underdamped under moderately hard cornering.

Predictably the Gold Wing's main problem came when all that weight had to be slowed down in a hurry. The brakes themselves, Japan's first triple-disc system, worked reasonably well, but using the front brake with the bike banked over even slightly put too much force through the steering head, resulting in a not-too-enjoyable twitch.

The GL1000's unsuitability for spirited riding was perhaps the main factor behind its mixed reception in Europe. But those factors mattered little to the older, touring-oriented American riders who rapidly adopted the smooth, quiet, and refined Gold Wing with such enthusiasm. The cult of the Gold Wing had arrived, and motorcycle touring would never be quite the same.

Not that these riders were totally happy with Honda's product,

Honda GL1000 Gold Wing (1976)

Engine type	Water-cooled SOHC, 8-valve flat four
Displacement	999cc
Bore x stroke	72 x 61.4 mm
Compression ratio	9.2:1
Carburetion	4 x 32 mm Keihins
Claimed power	80hp @ 7500 RPM
Transmission	5-speed
Electrics	12 V battery; 50/40 W headlamp
Frame	Tubular steel cradle
Front suspension	Telescopic, no adjustment
Rear suspension	Twin shock absorbers, adjustable preload
Front brake	Twin 280 mm (11 in) discs
Rear brake	290 mm (11.5 in) disc
Front tire	3.50 x 19 in
Rear tire	4.50 x 17 in
Wheelbase	1550 mm (61 in)
Seat height	800 mm (31.5 in)
Fuel capacity	19 liters (4.2 UK gal, 5 US gal)
Weight	290 kg wet (638 lb)

for they soon started modifying and decorating their GL1000s with a range of accessories, from fairings and luggage to extra chrome and lights. Honda initially made few modifications, though in 1978 the K3 model had a new seat, and used smaller carbs and revised valve timing to give some extra low-rev performance.

By the time the GL1100 Interstate (DX-B in Britain) arrived in 1980, adding a full fairing and hard luggage to the bigger 1085cc engine, new frame, and air-assisted suspension that had been introduced with the GL1100 earlier that year, more than 200,000 GL1000s had been sold worldwide. And the name Gold Wing had become synonymous with long-distance comfort and refinement.

Below: Straight-line cruising was always the big Honda's strength. Bottom left: The Gold Wing name soon became so popular that it was almost a brand in itself, leading to the creation of many owners' organizations worldwide. Bottom right: The original 999cc flat-four engine was tweaked with carburetion and valve timing mods in 1978, and grew to 1085cc two years later.

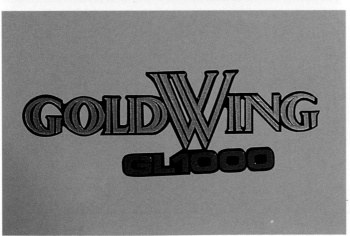

From *Cycle*, APR. 1975

"We don't know exactly how much the GL1000 is going to cost, but however much it turns out to be, it'll be a bargain in terms of utter engine smoothness and quietness, in terms of the quality of engineering and new-wave thinking that has gone into it, in terms of surprisingly agile handling performance, and shattering stopping and accelerating performance.

Here is a tourer, unblurred and brilliantly focused for those who want nothing to intrude on their feeling of the road and who want to intrude on no one else as they enjoy it."

From *Bike*, JAN. 1976

"When you start examining the Gold Wing's attributes as a tourer, it falls short on one or two important counts... It's an image bike, pure and simple. It ain't meant to be functional—it's just meant to swell your head.

The bike is perfectly capable, I'm sure, of cruising at a steady 110 mph [176 km/h]; only trouble is the rider isn't. Ten minutes at that sort of speed and you begin to feel the subject of some infernal mediaeval torture as the wind tries to wrench your arms from their sockets.

All that extra weight and complexity makes you wonder whether the advantages aren't outweighed by the penalties incurred."

Moto Morini 3½ Sport

With my chin on the fuel tank, the throttle wide open, and the little V-twin motor clattering away between my shins, the red-and-black Morini accelerated until its speedometer needle was almost touching the 100 mph (160 km/h) mark. The roundabout ahead got closer and closer... until finally I sat up and squeezed the brake lever, the bike slowed, and I trod down four gears with loud blips of the throttle before flicking the bike onto its side.

Cranking through the roundabout at an angle that would have had many old bikes gouging lumps out of the road, the Sport was untroubled. Its Pirellis stuck hard, nothing touched down, the suspension remained in control. And when the roundabout's exit appeared, I flicked the bars and nailed the throttle again to send the bike shooting out, revs climbing toward the 8000 RPM red-line as I kept the motor boiling with the closely spaced gearbox.

Few Seventies bikes are as fun to ride as the Moto Morini 3½ Sport. The little V-twin's combination of neat styling, agile handling, and rev-happy performance give much more appeal than its

capacity of just 344cc would suggest. In its day the Morini's high price—on a par with Honda's CB500-four and Suzuki's GT750 triple—prevented real sales success, but it made a big impression on all who rode it.

Like Ducati, Moto Morini was based in Bologna and became best known for V-twins after first producing small-capacity singles. Alfonso Morini had begun building bikes under the MM name in the 1920s, in partnership with Mario Mezzetti, and rode one himself to a class win in the 1927 Italian Grand Prix at Monza. After setting up under his own name following World War II, Morini built roadsters and successful racers, most notably the DOHC 250 on which Tarquinio Provini was runner-up in the 1963 world championship.

Opposite: The neat, chrome-plated exhaust heat shield and awkward, left-sided kick-start epitomize the Morini's blend of style and impracticality. Above: Few middleweights have ever looked as lean and aggressive as this Italian V-twin. Right: The Morini's racy riding position meant the "Sport" plate was hardly needed, but a neutral light would have come in handy.

The 3½ Sport was launched in 1974, and was one of two models powered by the air-cooled, 72-degree pushrod V-twin engine designed by Franco Lambertini. The basic 344cc model was the 3½ Strada, which had slightly raised bars, rounded styling, and a conventional dual-seat. Unusually, the engine featured Heron cylinder heads—flat-bottomed, with the combustion chamber in the concave piston crowns, and parallel valves.

Peak power output was a respectable 39 BHP at 8200 RPM, and the engine was very fuel efficient. Morini claimed the same output at a slightly higher 8500 RPM from the 3½ Sport, whose motor was identical apart from a hotter camshaft and different pistons that increased compression ratio to 11:1 from the Strada's 10:1. Other engine features shared by both models included electronic ignition, belt-driven camshaft, six-speed gearbox, plus a light and rigid chassis based around a steel twin-downtube frame.

Moto Morini 3½ Sport (1976)

Engine type	Air-cooled pushrod, 2-valve 72-degree V-twin
Displacement	344cc
Bore x stroke	62 x 57 mm
Compression ratio	11:1
Carburetion	2 x 25 mm Dell'Orto
Claimed power	39 BHP @ 8500 RPM
Transmission	6-speed
Electrics	12 V battery; 35/35 W headlamp
Frame	Tubular steel cradle
Front suspension	Telescopic, no adjustment
Rear suspension	Twin shock absorbers, adjustable preload
Front brake	Single 290 mm (11.4 in) disc
Rear brake	160 mm (6.3 in) SLS drum
Front tire	100/90 x 19 in
Rear tire	110/90 x 18 in
Wheelbase	1390 mm (54.7 in)
Seat height	787 mm (31 in)
Fuel capacity	16 liters (3.5 UK gal, 4.2 US gal)
Weight	153 kg (337 lb) wet

The more glamorous Sport's fuel tank was more angular than the Strada's, and like the side panels, was finished in red and black. Low clip-on handlebars and a racy humped seat gave a lean, aggressive look, which on early Sports was further enhanced by a huge, double-sided front drum brake. Early Stradas made do with a more modest single drum; this 1976-model Sport was fitted with the Grimeca front disc that was introduced to both models at around that time.

After locating the ignition key down by your left thigh, you flick up the choke levers of the 25 mm Dell'Orto carbs and swing the left-sided kick-starter to bring the little motor to life with a restrained bark. The Sport's riding position puts too much weight on your wrists and bum, and explains why many early Sports were fitted with rear-sets. But the bike feels low, slim, and light.

The V-twin doesn't much like low revs, vibrating slightly and spluttering when the throttle is wound back at 4000 RPM. But at about 5000 RPM the Sport comes alive, feeling better the faster it spins. The real power is between six grand and the 8500 RPM peak. Keep the V-twin spinning using the six-speed gearbox, and the Sport will maintain a fairly smooth 80 mph (130 km/h), stretching its legs from there toward a top speed of about 100 mph (160 km/h).

The need for frequent gearchanging made it important that the

Below left: The Sport lines up with its sensible sibling the 3½ Strada, whose upright riding position and softly tuned engine gave a more relaxed feel. Below right: Morini's 344cc V-twin engine held its cylinders at 72 degrees apart, and used unusual Heron cylinder heads. The Bologna firm also built a 500cc V-twin and later tried turbocharging, without success.

From *Bike*, MAY 1975

"The engine is very responsive and revs incredibly freely—almost like a two-stroke in fact. Its only demerits are a lack of usable power below about 3500 RPM and a wildly inaccurate tachometer. However, the Morini is blessed with a six-speed gearbox, which means you're never at a loss for sufficient horses.

Part of the reason for the Morini's accomplished road behavior was certainly due to the suspension arrangements; Marzocchi front and rear. There was a fair bit of travel in the front forks but they were progressively damped and the spring rate was clearly well matched to the Morini's weight.

Some folk may arguably resent paying out so many greenies for what is, after all, a 350 lightweight. But then the 3½ Sport probably has more power than such people will ever need... So to paraphrase Marie Antoinette, 'Let them ride Hondas!' "

six-speed box worked well, which it did at speed. Things weren't so clever at a standstill, when the Morini's curious lack of a neutral light sometimes meant I discovered a neutral between second and third—then stalled when I tried to pull away in second.

But such minor complaints are quickly forgotten when the sun's shining and you find a good winding road. This is a small, light bike whose 1390 mm (54.7 in) wheelbase and dry weight of less than 150 kg (330 lb) compare favorably with most modern sport machines—even if its old-fashioned steering geometry and 18-inch front wheel reveal its age. Stability was excellent, and the sharp-steering, well-suspended Morini went round corners effortlessly.

Other cycle parts were excellent, too. The single 290 mm (11.4 in) Grimeca front disc brake felt slightly spongy by modern standards, but it was capable of hauling the little Morini to a halt very sharply, aided by a small rear drum. And the Pirellis gripped well enough to make good use of the narrow Sport's ground clearance.

Of course the revvy Sport is a single-minded little machine offering a low level of comfort or practicality. In a straight line it was not particularly fast even in the mid-Seventies, and that is even more true now. But the Morini's blend of style and twisty-road performance surely qualify it for superbike status. On the right road, the V-twin is a blast, its revvy engine, excellent chas-

sis, and reputation for reliability encouraging you to ignore its age and ride it hard.

That makes the Morini a desirable little bike all these years later, as does the fact that the Sport is now much more affordable than when new. Morini owners tend to be real enthusiasts who stick with the marque for many years. When you ride a 3½ Sport, it's easy to see why.

Suzuki GT550A

I'll never forget my first ride on a Suzuki GT550A, and not just because it was the first nearly new motorbike I'd ever been on. It was also one of the most exciting and terrifying experiences of my life.

Not that I was actually *riding* the air-cooled triple back in 1976, you understand. I was merely the passenger, on the briefest of rides across a large car-park, aboard the Suzuki owned by our school's resident rich kid and motorbike fanatic.

This was one lucky schoolboy—the recipient of a screaming 50cc Yamaha FS1-E from his parents for his 16th birthday, a Suzuki GT185 for his 17th, and a GT550 to celebrate his 18th. He was posing with his gleaming triple outside the local disco one evening, casually dropping comments such as "ton-plus top speed" into the conversation with this easily impressed would-be motorcyclist. Then he said I could have a quick go on the back if I liked.

Seconds later I was perched on the pillion seat, the burble from the trio of two-stroke cylinders just about drowning out the *boom-boom-boom* of my heartbeat. It was the gentle way that he pulled away that threw me. I relaxed my grip on the grab-rail just as he

notched it into second, grabbed a handful of throttle, and sent the Suzuki screaming forward with a force that sent my legs in the air and, for several agonizing seconds, made me think I was about to be left in a heap on the ground.

Thankfully he had to back off moments later; I just stayed on, and naturally didn't admit afterwards that I'd been the slightest bit worried. I was certainly changed forever, though. It was probably during those few moments that I was incurably addicted to big, fast, hard-accelerating motorcycles.

And before you start sneering, back in 1976 that's exactly what the Suzuki GT550A was. The air-cooled two-stroke triple might not have had the cubes or the outright performance of Suzuki's water-cooled GT750-three, let alone the likes of Kawasaki's H2 750. But the 550's lively acceleration and genuine 100 mph-plus

Opposite: The air-cooled GT550 was a much slimmer and lighter machine than its better known stablemate, the liquid-cooled GT750. Above: The 550's profile was very similar to that of Suzuki's smaller GT380 triple. Right: Instrument console included a digital gear indicator and, more importantly, a speedo that indicated 100mph (160km/h) on a good day.

Suzuki GT550A (1976)

Engine type	Air-cooled two-stroke triple
Displacement	543cc
Bore x stroke	61 x 62 mm
Compression ratio	6.8:1
Carburetion	3 x 28 mm Mikunis
Claimed power	53 BHP @ 7500 RPM
Transmission	5-speed
Electrics	12 V battery; 50/40 W headlamp
Frame	Tubular steel twin cradle
Front suspension	Telescopic, no adjustment
Rear suspension	Twin shock absorbers, adjustable preload
Front brake	Single 300 mm (11.8 in) disc
Rear brake	178 mm (7 in) drum
Front tire	3.25 x 19 in
Rear tire	4.00 x 18 in
Wheelbase	1460 mm (57.5 in)
Seat height	825 mm (32.5 in)
Fuel capacity	15 liters (3.3 UK gal, 4 US gal)
Weight	205 kg (451 lb) wet

(160 km/h-plus) top speed meant that it was outclassed only by the fastest of superbikes.

The GT550, known as the Indy in the States, had been around since 1972, gaining a disc front brake, a few horsepower, and a few other improvements along the way. Similar in looks and layout to the GT380 triple, it was notable for employing Suzuki's Ram Air System—which referred to the simple piece of bent metal that helped direct a cooling breeze over the cylinder head. Breathing in through a trio of 28 mm Mikuni carburetors and out through a bulky four-pipe exhaust system, the 543cc motor produced 53 BHP at 7500 RPM.

A typical twin-cradle steel frame held nonadjustable forks and twin shocks with five-way preload adjustment. Rounded styling, a thick dual-seat and weight of 205 kg—pretty heavy by middle-weight standards—suggested a practical all-rounder in the style of the range-topping GT750. But although it was tall and roomy, this

nicely restored GT550 felt quite light and sporty as I hit the button, prodded it into gear, and set off.

The engine took no time at all to confirm just how torquey and relaxed it was. The Suzuki pulled away easily, and its pleasantly crisp midrange performance was well matched to the fairly relaxed pace encouraged by the wide, slightly raised handlebars. When I short-shifted through the slick five-speed gearbox, the GT550 responded with a steady stream of power.

At most revs the rubber-mounted triple felt reasonably smooth, too, though from about 5000 RPM it began to buzz through its bars and footpegs, before smoothing out again toward the red-line. Top speed was close to 110 mph (175 km/h). But on this windy day it wouldn't pull above an indicated 80 mph (130 km/h) in top, and only screamed to 95 mph (153 km/h) when I changed down to fourth to get the revs up nearer the 7500 RPM red-line.

That blustery wind also brought out the worst in the Suzuki's chassis, triggering a gentle wobble that began at about 80 mph (130 km/h) and refused to go away until I slowed down. But the bike never felt worrying, and its handling at slower speeds was pretty good, let down only by the overfirm suspension.

On smooth roads the GT could be cornered pretty rapidly, even so, aided by its narrow but respectably grippy Pirellis. Those wide bars gave enough leverage to allow fairly quick direction

changes, despite the old-fashioned steering geometry and 19-inch front wheel. Brakes were reasonably good, too, the Suzuki's single front disc slowing the bike hard with help from the cable-operated rear drum.

That all helped make the GT550 a deceptively rapid bike, and it was practical in some ways, too. Switchgear and instrumentation (including a digital gear indicator) were competent, the seat comfortable, and the solid grab-rail gave most pillions, at least, a chance of enjoying the ride. But the headlamp was feeble, and the motor so thirsty that the small fuel tank gave a range of only about 100 miles (160 km).

That and the harsh ride handicapped the GT550's touring ability and help explain why the bike was never as popular as Suzuki must have hoped. By 1976 the opposition from four-strokes such as Honda's new CB550-four was strong, while the triple had improved little in several years—partly because Suzuki knew that time was running out for smoky, thirsty two-strokes.

A year later, in 1977, Suzuki entered the four-stroke middleweight market with the GS550-four, leaving the two-stroke on the sidelines. Although the GS was more expensive and no faster than the GT, it looked and handled better, and was more economical, more environmentally friendly, and clearly the machine of the future. The GT550 triple's days were numbered, but for me and plenty of others, it had provided some memorable moments.

From *Bike*, Nov. 1976

"Lack of rear suspension compliance must be one of the Suzuki's worst points, along with a poor riding position and inadequate fuel capacity. Best thing about the rubber-mounted motor is its vast acreage of usable power, spread from anything over three grand right up to the red-line.

Even five gears seem one too many on occasion, so smooth is the urgent surge of three cylinders. But just as you're about to sail smoothly over the legal limit at 5000 RPM in top, an ugly patch of vibration shows up.

Its frame may look just like a collection of tubes holding two wheels apart, tacked together with aesthetically repulsive gusseting, but it handles despite the rear springs' attempts to prevent it holding a line. It may not wheelie its way into your affections, but a standing quarter time in the 13-second bracket from 543cc ain't to be sniffed at."

Moto Guzzi
Le Mans Mk 1

The speedo is indicating about 90 mph (145 km/h) as I roll back the throttle, select top gear with a deliberate prod of my left boot, and then tug the big Dell'Ortos open again to send the V-twin forward with renewed urge. With my head tucked as far as possible behind the tiny flyscreen, my ears are treated to a blend of sucking bellmouths, clattering valvegear, and rumbling exhausts as Moto Guzzi's 850 Le Mans accelerates with the lazy, long-legged feel that made it famous.

Many years have passed since the Le Mans was released, but time has barely diminished the thrill of unleashing this uniquely charismatic machine. Perhaps the only sensation missing now is the heady excitement, uppermost in a Le Mans rider's mind in 1976, of being aboard one of the very fastest bikes on the road.

The Le Mans was one of the quirkiest and finest of Seventies superbikes, as well as one of the most handsome. Its heart was the air-cooled, 90-degree V-twin motor whose pushrod-operated, two-valves-per-cylinder format still lives on at Mandello del Lario. The Le Mans' 844cc capacity came from enlarging the 750cc S3's motor to give dimensions of 83 x 78 mm. The new engine also benefited from a higher 10.2:1 compression ratio, bigger 36 mm Dell'Ortos, and new exhausts that combined to lift peak output to 80 BHP at 7300 RPM.

Several chassis parts were borrowed from the S3, including the twin-cradle steel frame and Guzzi's own forks. Brakes were by Brembo: three big 300 mm (11.8 in) discs operated via Guzzi's linked system that used the foot pedal to work one front caliper, as well as the rear.

Few vehicles of any kind have aged as gracefully as the Le Mans. The bike is a masterpiece of automotive art, from its rakish screen, through the way its fuel tank is embraced by the raised front of the angular seat, to its slatted side panels and upswept black silencers. And at the center is that big, bulging, distinctive

Opposite: Few mid-Seventies superbikes went round corners like the Le Mans, or looked remotely as stylish in the process. Above: Guzzi had built several sporty V-twins in previous years, but the Le Mans' bikini fairing and seat gave it a look all its own. Right: Big 36mm Dell'Orto carbs enhanced a V-twin engine that had grown to 844cc in capacity.

gray mass of an engine, muscular and powerful yet at the same time rounded and smooth.

My first impression of this immaculately restored Le Mans was simply how small it was. Although the bike is long, with a rangy 1511 mm (59.5 in) wheelbase, from that shapely seat it felt tiny. The clip-ons were within easy reach, angling back from a cockpit whose black-faced dials were largely obscured, because I'm tall, by the swept-back screen. The footrests were sufficiently forward and high to place my knees above the sticking-out pots.

When I hit the starter button there was a brief pause, then *whoomph* the motor fired, sending the bike lurching from side to side as the revs rose and fell, then settling to a steady tickover while the tach needle continued to dance across the dial. Few Italian bikes of the Seventies were free of such quirks, and the Guzzi's clutch was another, its grabbiness as I pulled away a hint

that the twin-plate unit was not the engine's strong point.

The gearchange was never too hot either, especially in the lower ratios, and even when I shifted the long-travel lever carefully it was easy to find a false neutral. But as the Le Mans loped away it was impossible not to be captivated by the gentle throbbing—too pleasant to be called vibration—of the big V-twin, and by the sounds coming from its pipes and from those gaping bellmouths down by my shins.

Low-speed acceleration was modest by modern standards, but the V-twin motor was impressively tractable, requiring a minimum of cog-swapping to keep it pulling urgently out of bends. And it came into its own at higher speeds, where simply rolling open the heavy-action throttle resulted in brisk action as the power pulses quickened, the various sounds intensified, and the Guzzi charged forward toward a top speed of a little over 130 mph (210 km/h).

That sort of speed was within the capability of several rivals, including Kawasaki's considerably cheaper Z900-four. But where the Le Mans scored was in its chassis' ability to handle all the engine could deliver. With the motor acting as a stressed member, frame rigidity was absolute. And the Guzzi's conservative steering geometry helped ensure high-speed stability with no need for the steering damper at its headstock, while the leaned-forward riding position and tiny flyscreen made fast cruising reasonably comfortable.

Admittedly, part of the Le Mans' handling secret was in the stiffness of its suspension. The forks in particular punished my wrists on rough roads, especially under heavy braking. The rear

Moto Guzzi Le Mans Mk 1 (1976)

Engine type	Air-cooled pushrod, 2-valve transverse V-twin
Displacement	844cc
Bore x stroke	83 x 78 mm
Compression ratio	10.2:1
Carburetion	2 x 36 mm Dell'Ortos
Claimed power	80 BHP @ 7300 RPM
Transmission	5-speed
Electrics	12 V battery; 45/40 W headlamp
Frame	Tubular steel cradle
Front suspension	Telescopic, no adjustment
Rear suspension	Twin Sebac shock absorbers, adjustable preload
Front brake	Twin 300 mm (11.8 in) Brembo discs
Rear brake	300 mm (11.8 in) Brembo disc (linked system)
Front tire	3.50 x 18 in
Rear tire	4.00 x 18 in
Wheelbase	1511 mm (59.5 in)
Seat height	743 mm (29.3 in)
Fuel capacity	23 liters (5 UK gal, 6 US gal)
Weight	216 kg (476 lb) wet

Below: Guzzi's attempts to develop the Le Mans were generally unsuccessful. The Le Mans II, introduced in 1978, had an angular full fairing based on that of the Spada tourer. It was more practical than the original model's smaller item, but far less stylish. Below right: Pirelli Phantoms were arguably the stickiest and best superbike tires in the Seventies, and despite lack of width still allow a Le Mans rider to make good use of the bike's generous ground clearance. Guzzi's linked brake system meant that one front disc was operated by hand, the other by foot along with the rear disc.

Sebacs also passed plenty of bumps through to the thin seat, though at least their lack of travel minimized the unsettling effect of the drive-shaft torque reaction if I opened or closed the throttle in a bend. Ground clearance was pretty good, as was the grip from the typically narrow Pirelli Phantoms on the 18-inch wheels.

Opinion on Guzzi's linked brake system was mixed even in the Le Mans' heyday, with many riders swearing by it but plenty of others unconvinced. The hand-operated disc was feeble on its own, and the need to use the foot pedal for all but the gentlest braking meant modifying my riding style to suit. But the trio of Brembo's finest gave plenty of stopping power when they were all hauled on in anger.

Other idiosyncrasies included a fiddly centerstand and hopelessly dim 45/40 W headlight. That racy riding position became painful in town, and I soon rediscovered Guzzi's hard-to-cancel indicator switch, which had me riding along flashing left-right-left in period fashion, just as I recall doing on my own T3 tourer years ago.

Such faults were all part of the Le Mans experience. And it's easy to forgive the old warrior when you ride it—or even when you simply feast your eyes on this, one of the most sensual of all Seventies superbikes. However long motorcycles are produced on the banks of Lake Lecco, it's debatable whether Moto Guzzi will build a machine more stylish and soulful than the original 850 Le Mans.

From *Bike*, Aug. 1977

"How can you be cold and objective about a bike that's so fine you go all weak at the knees just looking at it?

It's long and lean, all matte-black racing machismo and tastefully extrovert flamboyance. And it looks so potent: the dull grey bulk of those massive cylinders thrusting out from the lovely tank nestling between them, and the enormous carburetors flaunting great gaping velocity stacks.

A top speed of 132.15 mph [212.6 km/h] and a standing quarter time of 13.09 seconds make it the fastest production bike we've ever put through our electronic speed trap. High speed stability is so good that I left the hydraulic steering damper in the off position all the time, and yet the bike was rock steady—even at 130 mph [209 km/h] when bumps on our test track were bucking the rear wheel into the air."

Harley-Davidson XLCR1000

The city streets were thick with traffic, but it was still a memorable ride. With deceptive speed, the slim black Harley carved a swathe through the slow-moving metal. The slightest twist of throttle sent the torquey V-twin stomping effortlessly forward. Everywhere the XLCR went, its booming bass exhaust note cleared cars from its path and threatened to turn buildings to rubble.

Magical stuff—and I wasn't even riding the Harley, just following behind on a modern Honda while the XLCR's owner led the way through his local patch with practiced ease. Even before I got to ride it, the original Harley-Davidson Café Racer had charmed me with its unique style and presence. But if that's the XLCR's great strength, then it's also the bike's fatal flaw. If ever a motorcycle was built for image rather than performance, this 1977 machine is the one.

The Café Racer concept was dreamt up by Harley design chief Willie G. Davidson, and he took the idea to the limit. Almost every component was black: the bikini fairing, fuel tank, tapered flat-track–style seat unit, side panels, fenders, frame, exhaust system,

and most of all, the big 45-degree V-twin engine itself.

Beneath the styling, the XLCR was rather less exotic. Its engine was the same four-speed, 998cc pushrod unit used in the Sportster, with not a hot cam or big valve to be seen. Compression ratio remained a modest 9:1, and even the 38 mm Keihin carb was identical. The Café Racer's one novelty, its siamesed black exhaust system, made no difference to the peak output of 61 BHP at 6200 RPM.

The black bike's frame was a new design, consisting of a Sportster front section, matched with rear tubes and a box-section swingarm based on those of the XR750 racebike. Geometry and the 1486 mm (58.5 in) wheelbase were identical to those of the Sportster, though the Café Racer's triple-disc brake system was an

Opposite: Harley's big 45-degree V-twin engine had black barrels, a siamesed exhaust system, and, in this bike's case, an aftermarket S&S carburetor and air filter. Above: Bikini fairing, black finish, and lean styling justified the café racer tag, even if performance didn't. Right: Screen and flat handlebars meant that the rider's view was nothing like that provided by other Harleys.

upgrade from that bike's single disc, rear drum combination.

If that and the black bike's racy lines conspired to give the impression of a hard and fast street scratcher, then the riding position prompted a few doubts. That was certainly true as I threw a leg over the low seat and leant forward not to clip-ons, but to near-straight bars. Although the footpegs were rear-set, they were no higher than those of the Sportster. Combined with the XLCR's taller seat, that gave a generous amount of legroom.

At the press of the starter button, those massive 81 mm (3.2 in) diameter pistons began thudding up and down on their shared crankpin with a loud, offbeat note that could only come from a Harley. And when I trod into gear and let out the clutch, the CR pulled away with all the traditional tractor-like ease of a big motor that thumped out peak torque at just 3800 RPM.

This Café Racer was well used and unrestored, with the slightly

Harley-Davidson XLCR1000 (1977)

Engine type	Air-cooled pushrod, 2-valve 45-degree V-twin
Displacement	998cc
Bore x stroke	81 x 96.8 mm
Compression ratio	9:1
Carburetion	38 mm Keihin (original; this bike S&S)
Claimed power	61 BHP @ 6200 RPM
Transmission	4-speed
Electrics	12 V battery; 45/35 W headlamp
Frame	Tubular steel twin cradle
Front suspension	Telescopic, no adjustment
Rear suspension	Twin shock absorbers, adjustable preload
Front brake	Twin 254 mm (10 in) discs
Rear brake	254 mm (10 in) disc
Front tire	3.75 x 19 in
Rear tire	4.25 x 18 in
Wheelbase	1486 mm (58.5 in)
Seat height	787 mm (31 in)
Fuel capacity	11 liters (2.4 UK gal, 2.9 US gal)
Weight	234 kg (515 lb) wet

lived-in appearance—a few chips in the paintwork, slightly tarnished pipes and alloy—inevitable after 23,000 miles (37,000 km). Apart from a Screamin' Eagle fork brace and S&S carb and filter, it was standard.

Contemporary road tests rated the Café Racer less strong than the standard XLCH 1000 below 3000 RPM, although that unequal-length exhaust system, which was claimed to boost midrange power, was the only difference between the two models. It's hard to say whether the aftermarket carb helped, but this bike pulled well from below 2500 RPM even in top.

Throttle response was generally crisp, and the Hog stomped forward eagerly, its low-rev torque encouraging short-shifting through the rather sluggish four-speed box. Back in '77 the Café Racer's top speed was close to the 120 mph (195 km/h) mark that Harley claimed, though the solid-mounted motor's inevitable vibration was another good reason for concentrating on the lower part of the rev range.

A quick burst up to about 90 mph (145 km/h) was enough to prove that this wild boar could still charge hard, but I wouldn't have wanted to keep that pace up for long. Although an indicated 70 mph (113 km/h) came up with just 3500 RPM showing on the tach in top, vibration started getting tiresome at much above those revs, swiftly followed by pain from the thin single seat.

Handling was rated as acceptable when the bike was new, although the Harley needed a hefty haul on its narrow bars to steer its considerable bulk around tight bends. Above 80 mph (130 km/h) this bike's bars began to deliver a distinctly vague feel, probably provoked by the unhelpful aerodynamics of the handlebar-mounted fairing. Contemporary tests reported a weave at speeds above 90 mph (145 km/h), with the spindly twin-downtube frame being another suspect.

This bike's blend of Michelin front and Metzeler rear tires doubtless gave considerably more grip than the original rubber (generally Goodyears), although I didn't push hard enough to confirm reports that the gearlever was the first thing to touch down in left-handers. I did use the brakes hard, though, and I needed to because the twin-disc front setup was very wooden,

From *SuperBike*, JUN. 1972

"Harley-Davidson's XLCR (pronounced Excelsior—how else?) is a once-in-a-lifetime machine. Hunched and low, it's nonetheless massive and mighty. It bellows like a medieval monster. It pulls like a freight train. And it looks like a midnight fantasy—black, malevolent, a loner's one-man escape route to the plains of solitude.

Look at it coldly and it becomes, if not mediocre, certainly less than the paragon some people expect. It's not madly fast—though it'll hit 120 and bellow off the line with wheel-spinning ferocity; the engine's rough; the finish a touch crude; and much of the engineering bloody agricultural. Thing is, you can't examine a Harley coldly. It positively reeks of passion.

Big Black is the most anachronistic superbike around... Rumor has it that the guy who invented the wheel is alive and well and living in Milwaukee. Long may they continue to build *real* bikes like the XLCR."

despite receiving considerable praise in '77.

Testers then were more keen to criticize the feeble headlamp, drag-prone clutch, and leaky fuel cap. But those faults did not stop them enthusing about the style and class of a machine that, as one put it, stood out in a world of mass-produced standardization like a hooker at a convent school speech day.

Unfortunately for Harley, the public was not convinced. The XLCR appealed neither to genuine sports riders not to the traditional Harley crowd. If the CR was notable for anything, it was for proving that there was more to a sportbike than slick styling and a few chassis mods.

But of course all that doesn't matter any more. What counts now is that Willie G's grand folly is still just as black, loud, and mean as it ever was. All these years later, the XLCR's looks, noise, and charisma more than make up for the fact that it never really was a true Café Racer at all.

Suzuki GS750

One moment the sun was shining, the next the sky had turned black and my promise to return the GS750 in the condition I'd borrowed it was looking very rash. With less than a mile (1.6 km) to go the heavens opened, instantly soaking both the Suzuki and me—and bringing the memories flooding back. Suddenly it was 1977, and I was riding a friend's nearly new blue GS, for the first time, through a similar downpour.

At the time, the GS wasn't just by far the best bike I'd ridden, it was arguably the most competent superbike on the roads. And boy, was it fast! (Especially to someone whose own bike was an old Triumph twin.) I can still vividly remember crouching forward into the rain, with my feet on the pillion pegs, and glancing down to see the speedo needle reading an incredible 125 mph (200 km/h)—about 25 mph (40 km/h) faster than I'd ever been before in my life.

To say that I was impressed with the GS750 that day was an understatement, and I was by no means the only rider to be overwhelmed by the four-cylinder Suzuki's brilliant blend of power, han-dling, and all-around ability. The concept of a light-heavyweight four was by no means new in those days, of course. Honda's CB750 had been around for eight years, and in 1977 Kawasaki's reputation for big fours, forged by the Z1 and its descendants, had just been enhanced by the arrival of the Z650.

In contrast, the GS was the first big four-stroke from Suzuki. In typical Japanese style, what Suzuki's engineers had done was study the opposition's products, draw up a very similar design containing some clever refinements of their own—and produce a machine that was in many ways the best big four of the lot.

The twin-cam, eight-valve motor they came up with was very similar to that of Kawasaki's Z1/Z900, even sharing the Kawa's valve sizes and 66 mm bore, with a reduced 56.4 mm stroke giving a

Opposite: Like many Seventies superbikes, the GS750 had flat handlebars in Europe and higher ones, as with this example, for the US market. Above: Styling of Suzuki's first big four-stroke was pleasant rather than exciting. The same couldn't be said of its staggering performance. Right: With a following wind, an indicated 125mph (200km/h) was temptingly easy.

capacity of 748cc. Its only real innovation was an automatic cam-chain tensioner that, like the rest of the motor, would prove commendably reliable. Breathing in through a bank of 26 mm Mikuni carbs and out through a suitably restrained twin-pipe exhaust system, the GS unit produced a class-leading 68 BHP at 8500 RPM.

In a similar vein, there was nothing unusual about the Suzuki's chassis, with its familiar format of twin-downtube steel frame, simple forks, and preload-adjustable twin shocks. Like the engine, though, the GS chassis had been thoughtfully designed, with a well-braced steering head area, plus needle-roller bearings for the swingarm. And although the GS didn't turn many heads with its styling, it was pleasant in an understated way.

I'd ridden a GS only once since that memorable first blast, but the Suzuki's typical layout, with a fairly upright riding position and tall, wide dual-seat, made me feel instantly at home. (European market bikes had flatter handlebars than this US-spec machine.) So did the air-cooled engine's anonymous blend of mechanical rustle and muted exhaust note, after I'd pulled out the steering-head–mounted choke knob and hit the starter button.

An excess of character was never something the GS was accused of possessing, but few owners complained about that. The Suzuki couldn't quite match the pace of Kawasaki's Z1000, but it was quicker than Honda's CB750 and Yamaha's XS750. This bike's motor felt nowhere near as potent as it must have when the GS

Full 45° banking angle and tucked-in exhaust system enables you to unwind bends with ease.

Right: Good quality shocks and needle-roller swingarm bearings contributed to the Suzuki's cornering ability. A grabby rear disc brake was one of its few chassis-related flaws. Below right: The leverage from this GS's high bars meant it could be flicked into turns with little effort, despite its Seventies-style relaxed steering geometry and 19-inch front wheel.

was new, but the air-cooled four's broad spread of power and slick five-speed gearbox still impressed. The Suzuki pulled cleanly from as low as 30 mph (50 km/h) in top gear, its generous midrange torque making for effortless overtaking.

And when the old bike was revved a bit harder, it responded with fondly remembered enthusiasm, kicking slightly at about 6000 RPM and surging toward the nine-grand red-line. Genuine top speed was a touch over 120 mph (195 km/h), but more importantly, the Suzuki cruised effortlessly at 90 mph (145 km/h). Although there was a typical and slight four-cylinder tingle at most engine speeds, the motor remained basically smooth however hard it was worked. In Seventies style, this was a sporty machine that was versatile enough to excel at commuting and touring, too.

Handling was regarded as one of the GS750's main attributes back in 1977, but I hadn't expected this bike to feel as good as it

Suzuki GS750 (1977)

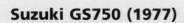

Engine type	Air-cooled DOHC, 8-valve transverse four
Displacement	748cc
Bore x stroke	65 x 56.4 mm
Compression ratio	8.7:1
Carburetion	4 x 26 mm Mikunis
Claimed power	68 BHP @ 8500 RPM
Transmission	5-speed
Electrics	12 V battery; 50/40 W headlamp
Frame	Tubular steel twin cradle
Front suspension	Telescopic, no adjustment
Rear suspension	Twin shock absorbers, adjustable preload
Front brake	Single 292 mm (11.5 in) disc
Rear brake	Single 292 mm (11.5 in) disc
Front tire	3.25 x 19 in
Rear tire	4.00 x 18 in
Wheelbase	1500 mm (59 in)
Seat height	787 mm (31 in)
Fuel capacity	18 liters (4 UK gal, 4.7 US gal)
Weight	232 kg (510 lb) wet

did all these years later. Although it was a fairly big and heavy machine, with a long, 1500 mm (59 in) wheelbase, typically old-fashioned chassis geometry, and a 19-inch front wheel, the GS seemed to shed much of its weight on the move. Steering was inevitably ponderous by modern standards, but given enough effort the Suzuki could be tipped into corners with satisfying speed, and it felt reassuringly neutral once into a bend.

From *SuperBike*, Jul. 1977

"Proper snake in the grass, that's the new Suzuki. It's sneaked up from behind, from a lair of softy strokers, to zap the opposition with such venom that they'll never be the same again. Using the technology pioneered by others, Suzuki have improved and refined, and quietly outclassed them all.

Not that you'd ever expect Suzuki's first four-stroke to be such an exciting bike. The GS750 looks, sounds and has the character of an especially well sorted vacuum cleaner. It's well mannered and unostentatious to the point of being a bit dull: the complete committee-designed consumer appliance.

Then you let the revs stray towards the upper reaches and suddenly the Suzuki transforms into a real superbike. What's more, the performance of frame, suspension and brakes are a match for this unexpected and extravagant metamorphosis. The GS has equally unexpected if less generous reserves of high-speed capability. It's an all-round speedster with few peers."

The GS's suspension, regarded as excellent in its day, felt slightly vague and crude at times. But it gave a comfortable ride, and for reasonably gentle use the Suzuki was fine, wallowing slightly only when asked to perform high-speed cornering feats for which even some modern retro-bikes would have been ill suited.

My only real chassis-related complaint concerned the brake system, which consisted of a single 292 mm (11.5 in) disc at each end. The front lacked power, needing a viselike grip on the lever for serious stopping. And the rear system, like many others of the time, was too sharp, locking up the wheel unless great care was taken with the right boot. A second front disc was added, along with cast wheels, in 1979.

Apart from that and some fresh color schemes, the model was unchanged—simply because no major modifications were required. The GS lasted three years (before being replaced by the faster but ill-handling 16-valve GSX750), and represented the start of great things for Suzuki. Those four-stroke engineers certainly got it right the first time with the GS750.

Bimota SB2

Chasing the setting sun to get the SB2 home before dark provided an excuse for a last, fast ride—and the perfect opportunity for the Bimota to show its class. It carved through the narrow, winding lanes with great poise. Then, when the road opened out, the bike showed its pure speed, pushing me back in the single seat as it stormed toward a top speed of over 130 mph (209 km/h). The miles flew past and soon the SB2 was back with its owner, just as the sun dipped below the horizon.

Such performance is nothing special by modern standards, but motorcycling was very different in 1977, when this Bimota was built. Back then such speed and agility from a roadgoing superbike were just a dream—unless you were one of the fortunate few owners of an SB2. Created with pure performance its only criterion, the Bimota was the most exotic and advanced sporting roadster of its age.

The SB2's brilliance is more easy to understand when you realize that this, the first ever Bimota streetbike, was designed by none other than Massimo Tamburini, architect of the Ducati 916 and

MV Agusta 750 F4. Tamburini was then the "Ta" of Bimota, the Rimini firm that he had founded in 1966 (initially to make heating and air-conditioning units) with Messrs Bianchi and Morri.

The maestro's signature is plain in the SB2. The Bimota's styling is as dramatic, if less sleek, as that of the 916 and F4. And like those bikes, the SB2, powered by the four-cylinder engine from Suzuki's GS750, backs up its radical look with a beautiful and advanced chassis incorporating steel frame tubes, state-of-the-art cycle parts, and an abundance of stylish details.

Chassis engineering was Bimota's specialty from its earliest motorcycling days. The first ever Bimota bike, the HB1 of 1972, was a Honda CB750-powered machine built for that year's Imola

Opposite: The SB2 went round corners better than any other production streetbike in 1977. Above: The uniquely streamlined Bimota was so advanced that it could almost have been built in the Nineties, not the Seventies. Right: Rubber catches (lower left) helped secure the tank cover. Conical couplings allowed the steel frame to be split for engine removal.

200-mile (322 km) race. The firm provided the chassis for the Yamaha on which Johnny Cecotto won the 350cc world championship in 1975, and the Harley-Davidsons that Walter Villa rode to both 250 and 350cc titles in the following season.

Tamburini's SB2 frame was made of chrome-molybdenum steel tubing of varying diameters. It had a heavily braced steering head area, used the engine as a stressed member, weighed just 10 kg (22 lb), and featured conical couplings that enabled the front and rear frame sections to be split, allowing rapid engine removal. Steering geometry could be adjusted by rotating eccentric bearings in the yokes. The Bimota also held its fork legs at a different angle to the steering head (28 degrees the forks, 24 the head) to reduce the change in trail under braking.

Bold engineering was equally in evidence at the rear of the chassis, where the Bimota was among the first roadbikes to use a single-shock rear suspension system. The swingarm was a long, box-section steel structure that curved outward to pivot concentric with the final drive sprocket, maintaining constant chain tension. Fork yokes, foot controls, and rear brake caliper carrier were machined from aircraft-grade aluminum alloy.

Tamburini also spared no expense in his specification for the cycle parts, which included 35 mm Ceriani forks with internals modified by Bimota, five-spoke magnesium wheels in 18-inch diameters, drilled Brembo discs gripped by twin-piston calipers, and a De Carbon rear shock.

If the Bimota's chassis was advanced, then its sculpted tank/seat unit was no less so. In the style of a modern grand prix racebike, the SB2's rear section is self-supporting, requiring no subframe. Release two rubber straps, unplug an electrical connector and the fuel pipe, and it can be lifted off, its weight giving away the fact that it's made not of carbon fiber but of fiberglass lined with aluminum. Even so, the Bimota weighed just 198 kg (436 lb) with an empty tank—almost 30 kg (66 lb) less than the standard GS750.

This bike also had considerably more power, thanks to tuning modifications that were typical of the time. Unfiltered, 29 mm Mikuni carbs replaced the standard 26 mm units; the exhaust system was a free-breathing four-into-one. The motor was bored out to 850cc and fitted with high-compression Yoshimura pistons. A gas-flowed cylinder head and Yoshimura Stage 3 camshafts helped increase rear-wheel output to a dyno-tested peak of 78 BHP at 9000 RPM, compared to about 60 BHP from the standard Suzuki.

It was the SB2's chassis that made the most vivid impression, though, from the moment I threw a leg over the brown suede seat. The Bimota is compact by Seventies standards, with a short wheelbase, low clip-on bars, and high, rear-set footrests. Even with its headstock in the steeper of its two positions, the SB2 was not quick-steering by modern standards, but it flicked through a left-right sequence given only moderate pressure on the clip-ons.

The response was very neutral, and the Bimota's firm, well-controlled suspension kept the bike stable as the pace got hotter.

Braking from the pair of drilled front Brembos was good, too, albeit lacking the power of most modern systems. This bike wore Dunlop K391 Endurance tires, which gave plenty of grip when I began exploring the generous ground clearance that Tamburini provided by raising its engine 25 mm higher than in the standard GS750.

The modified Suzuki motor provided enough punch to make life interesting on the straights, too. Power output dipped at around 5000 RPM, but once into its stride the Yoshimura-tuned engine sent the Bimota howling forward. An indicated 100 mph (160 km/h) was effortless, thanks partly to the efficient fairing. On a twisty road it was easy to keep the SB2 pulling hard by flicking through the five-speed gearbox.

Sadly for enthusiasts in 1977, the Bimota's price matched its performance and exotic nature all too well. It cost as much as *three* standard GS750s, with the result that fewer than 70 SB2s

Bimota SB2 (1977)

Engine type	Air-cooled DOHC, 8-valve transverse four (Suzuki GS750)
Displacement	843cc
Bore x stroke	69 x 56.4 mm
Compression ratio	9.5:1
Carburetion	4 x 39 mm Mikunis
ClaimedPower	78.3 BHP @ 9000 RPM
Transmission	5-speed
Electrics	12 V battery
Frame	Chrome-molybdenum steel
Front suspension	Ceriani telescopic
Rear suspension	Vertical monoshock, adjustable preload
Front brake	Twin 295 mm (11.6 in) Brembo discs
Rear brake	250 mm (9.8 in) disc
Front tire	100/90 x 18 in
Rear tire	130/80 x 18 in
Wheelbase	1390 mm (54.7 in)
Seat height	743 mm (29 in)
Fuel capacity	20 liters (4.4 UK gal, 5.3 US gal)
Weight	198 kg (436 lb) dry

were built. Subsequent Bimota roadsters, notably the Z1000-engined KB1 released a year later, featured plainer bodywork and a slightly less elaborate chassis to reduce costs.

All of which only goes to make this, the first and most outrageous Bimota sportster of all, even more special. It's doubtful whether Massimo Tamburini or anyone else has ever created a roadster with quite such a purposeful nature as the SB2. Or one that—in style, engineering, and performance—was so far ahead of its opposition.

From *Cycle* , 1977

"Its suspension settings, its weight distribution, its geometry, its wheelbase length, its cornering clearance and the strength of its frame all work together to provide handling response and stability that's beyond our critical expertise.

As hard as we could ride it, on the fastest, meanest roads we could find, it remained at the end what all of its technical ornamentation promised at the beginning: perfect."

Above left: The SB2 was typical of early Bimotas in having a swingarm that was designed to pivot on the same axis as the front sprocket, so the drive chain was not stressed by rear suspension movement. Above: The standard Suzuki instrument panel shares cockpit space with Bimota's lightweight top triple clamp. Adjustable steering geometry was yet another advanced chassis feature.

Yamaha XS750

Cruising along on a sweet-running XS750 as the sun sank lower in the sky at the end of a long day, it was easy to understand why so many riders had fallen in love with this bike almost a quarter of a century ago. The three-cylinder Yamaha purred along, feeling smooth and relaxed, and a generous amount of acceleration was readily available whenever I wound back the throttle.

At speeds up to 85 mph (137 km/h) the silver triple held the road with no hint of a weave, and it floated through bends with a poise that belied its considerable weight and age. The slightly leaned forward riding position and generous seat combined with a compliant suspension to keep me comfortable. Even details such as the self-canceling indicators gave the impression of a slick, well-finished superbike.

That's just how Yamaha's first big four-stroke multi seemed to those lucky enough to ride it back in 1977. Press and public alike raved about the XS, and plenty of customers were tempted by the combination of 120 mph (193 km/h) performance, Japanese engineering, shaft final drive, and very competitive price.

And then it all began to go wrong. Sadly for Yamaha and those who had bought the big triple, mechanical problems soon became apparent: a fast-wearing primary drive chain, piston ring trouble due to use of incorrect material, seizure of the middle cylinder if the oil was not kept very precisely topped up, and even a gearbox with a tendency to drop from fourth directly into first!

Word of those expensive troubles soon spread, and the XS750's sales slumped—which was a shame because the basic design was sound, and given more development the bike could have been a lasting success. With its cast alloy wheels, triple disc brakes, and stylish matte black engine, the Yam was a rapid and well-equipped machine that could cover long distances in comfort and style.

Its combination of three inline cylinders and shaft final drive

Opposite: Yamaha's 747cc dohc triple engine performed well and provided a welcome alternative to rival fours—until it started giving problems. Above: The triple's rounded styling also helped to set it apart from rival fours. Right: Shaft final drive added weight but was a useful feature, as superbike drive chain life was short in the Seventies.

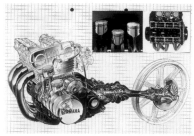

was unique, and Yamaha's engineers cleverly managed to incorporate the bevel gears necessary for the drive shaft while keeping the motor compact. The 747cc motor boasted twin overhead cams, a 120-degree crankshaft, and a fairly low 8.5:1 compression ratio. It produced a respectable maximum of 64 BHP at 7200 RPM.

Like most rivals, the XS had a steel twin-downtube frame, which held nonadjustable forks and a pair of rear shocks with five-way adjustable preload. With a claimed dry weight of 233 kg (512 lb), the XS was heavy even by the standards of the day. But despite that and the fairly tall, wide seat, the Yamaha felt very manageable as I climbed aboard and hit the button, ignoring the additional kick-starter.

When I pulled away I was instantly struck by the motor's smoothness and flexibility. The Yam's trio of CV Mikuni carbs gave glitch-free acceleration almost from tickover, and the bike

Yamaha XS750 (1977)

Engine type	Air-cooled DOHC, 6-valve transverse triple
Displacement	747cc
Bore x stroke	68 x 68.6 mm
Compression ratio	8.5:1
Carburetion	3 x 34 mm Mikunis
Claimed power	64 BHP @ 7200 RPM
Transmission	5-speed
Electrics	12 V 14Ah battery; 50/40W headlamp
Frame	Tubular steel twin cradle
Front suspension	Telescopic, no adjustment
Rear suspension	Twin shock absorbers, adjustable preload
Front brake	Twin 270 mm (10.6 in) discs
Rear brake	Single 270 mm (10.6 in) disc
Front tire	3.25 x 19 in
Rear tire	4.00 x 18 in
Wheelbase	1486 mm (57.8 in)
Seat height	826 mm (32.5 in)
Fuel capacity	17 liters (3.7 UK gal, 4.5 US gal)
Weight	233 kg dry (512 lb)

could be tricked down to 30 mph (48 km/h) in top gear without complaint—then catapulted forward at a decent rate given a simple tweak of the throttle.

Midrange response was pretty good, too, and on a flat road the triple would cruise at an indicated 100 mph (160 km/h) or just over with ease. Top gear was rather tall, so in the normal upright riding position the bike wouldn't rev out, and it was generally reluctant to do more than about 105 mph (168 km/h). But by wearing one-piece leathers and crawling under the tank paint, the testers of the day managed to get it to the red-line and a genuine 120 mph (193 km/h).

Being aware of the triple's mechanical reputation, I was reluctant to rev it too hard, which helped make for a pretty smooth ride. Apart from its lack of wind-protection, this felt like a bike that would cover serious distances in comfort, although even the most enthusiastic Seventies testers complained that its small fuel tank limited range to 140 miles (225 km) or less.

A few contemporary reports also mentioned a bit of twitchiness in bends, especially when the tires were worn, but despite this bike's age it was easy to see why handling was generally rated highly. The XS was a big, heavy bike that needed a fair effort to make it change course. But its size and lazy geometry combined with a strong frame and well-damped suspension to give a minimum of wobbles and weaves.

By modern standards the front brake setup of twin 270 mm (10.6 in) discs and single-pot calipers required a very hefty tug on the lever to make the Yamaha stop remotely hard, but by Seventies standards braking was good—at least in the dry. The poor wet-weather performance of tires and brakes, the small tank, and dim headlight were among the few criticisms aimed at the XS750 when new. But it didn't take long for word to get out that the XS750's engine and gearbox couldn't be trusted.

Yamaha cured a problem of premature wear of the ignition points by specifying electronic ignition for the XS750E model in 1978, and sorted out the other mechanical ailments with a variety of warranty recalls. The 750E also had an increase in peak power to 68 BHP at 8000 RPM, slightly shorter gearing, an uprated lubrication system, and preload-adjustable front forks. A year later the final 750F version added a larger but less attractive gas tank.

Even before that, the triple had been praised by one tester as "The Answer to practical motorcycling... a complete motorcycle that looks good, functions superbly and doesn't even cost too much." But the general public thought otherwise. Most riders preferred to stick to more reliable rival fours, and that remained true in 1980 when Yamaha enlarged the motor to 836cc and made numerous other changes to create the XS850.

All these years later an XS750 such as this one, well preserved

From *Motorcyclist*, SEP. 1976

"They could have just as easily have made it a four—probably easier in many respects—but the market is rapidly being flooded with fours, or soon will be in a couple of months when Suzuki and Kawasaki have finished doing their thing, and the hyper-innovative Yamahans obviously weren't convinced that's where it's at. Not when they could build a narrower engine that is much, much quieter, has fewer moving parts, more usable mid-range torque and equal smoothness.

Conceptually the XS750 is more of a heavy cruiser than a scalding racer; had they wanted that image they would have gone to at least a 900.

The engine is the main feature of the XS750 show; I think you're going to eat it up. Muscular, unprecedentedly quiet and good looking, this three is virtually immune to hard labor. Especially strong low- and mid-range power characteristics provide highway acceleration and passing ability identical to the Honda fours, including the GL1000."

and with its problems sorted, is a very pleasant bike to ride. But the moral of its story is simple: to build a great superbike, you must first of all make it reliable.

1978

Honda CBX1000

After all this time you'd think its impact would be dulled, but that magnificent motor still hits you between the eyes like a sledgehammer. Despite all the years that have passed since the CBX1000 was unleashed, it's debatable whether any bike since has matched the sheer visual force of the six.

Honda's mighty machine seems even more outrageous these days, when high-performance bikes hide their powerplants behind fairings, than it did when it first appeared in 1978. Naked bikes may be common but they look insignificant alongside that angled-forward apartment block with its bank of shiny downpipes. (As did Benelli's earlier 750 Sei, with its smaller six-pot powerplant.)

The CBX flaunts raw horsepower and technology in a manner that no modern machine can match, and its styling has a timeless quality that seems as fresh today as ever before. Apart from an incongruously dated front-end—whose skinny fork legs, tiny brake discs, and narrow tire make the CBX look like a heavyweight boxer with a model-girl's arms—the Honda is a bike that any current designer would surely kill to have produced.

And the secret of the CBX's lasting appeal is that its beauty is by no means merely skin deep. The six backed-up its appearance—and the discordantly discreet "Super Sport" logo on its tank—by going straight to the top of the performance charts, with a top speed approaching 140 mph (225 km/h), plus handling, roadholding, and braking that were all excellent by the standards of the day.

The CBX1000 had its roots in contrasting periods of Honda's history. First was the mid-Sixties grand prix era, when a young engineer named Shoichiro Irimajiri designed a series of high-revving four-strokes raced by riders such as Mike Hailwood, Ralph Bryans, and Luigi Taveri. Honda quit racing at the end of 1967, and the next decade was far less glorious on the track and in the showroom.

Opposite: Despite the inevitable width of the CBX's cylinders, Honda made room for the rider's legs by locating the alternator above the gearbox, and angling the six carbs inward in two banks of three. Above: The CBX looked like nothing else on the road in 1978—and it had the performance to match. Right: Engine protector bars were a popular accessory, for obvious reasons.

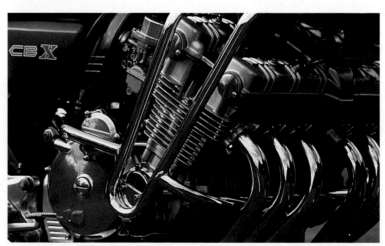

The CBX project was sparked by Honda's desire for a machine to put the company back at the forefront of motorcycle design. Four- and six-cylinder designs were considered before the six's character and heritage won the day. "When we were racing," Irimajiri later said, "we were up against the four-cylinder two-strokes of Yamaha and Suzuki. Cylinder multiplication was the only way we could be competitive. The CBX is a direct descendent of those race engines."

The 1047cc CBX did not rev to anything like the speed of the racers (Hailwood's 250-6 gave 53 BHP at 16,500 RPM), its 105 BHP maximum being produced at 9000 RPM. But many details were adapted, notably in the cylinder head, which used buckets and shims to work the 24 valves. A Hy-Vo chain turned the hollow, two-piece exhaust cam, with another chain running from that to the inlets. The CBX trod new ground by using magnesium for several engine covers.

Engine width was a potential problem. Legroom was provided for the rider by tilting the cylinders forward by 33 degrees, and by angling the six carbs inward in two banks of three. A jackshaft, above the gearbox and driven by chain, carried the alternator and ignition system, allowing the six to be only 50 mm (2 in) wider than Honda's CB750 unit.

Weight was reduced with aluminum handlebars and plastic mudguards. With the Gold Wing around to satisfy touring riders, Honda went flat-out to make the CBX a sports machine. Best of all, the bike was styled with a simple elegance that made the most of the unique engine by hanging it out in the wind with no frame tubes to spoil the visual effect.

This immaculately preserved CBX felt almost new as I pressed the starter button and the motor burbled smoothly into life. Even at slow speed, riding the six is an experience. The black-faced clocks and clip-on bars seem classy, the riding position is sportily leaned-forward, controls are light, and throttle response instant. The motor was so tractable that when I cracked open the Keihins from 2000 RPM in top, the Honda leapt forward without so much as a hiccup.

It was best to make use of the lower ratios, though, to savor the moment when the tach needle reached 6000 RPM and the six came alive. The CBX stretched its legs and headed for the horizon, the exhaust note hardening to a soulful yowl. In an instant I was traveling at over 90 mph (145 km/h), gripping the bars tightly as the roadside hedges turned into a blur and the tarmac seemed increasingly twisty.

Inevitably the CBX's chassis shows its age more than the engine, and by modern standards the forks and FVQ shocks felt harsh. Brakes were much-praised at the time, but the front stopper had nothing like the bite of a modern setup. And the ground clearance, though originally rated good, was easily used up thanks to Michelin tires that gave more grip than was available when the bike was new.

Not surprisingly, press reaction in 1978 was ecstatic. The engine was rated a masterpiece for its blend of smoothness and acceleration. Handling was deemed very acceptable, despite some stability problems when the tires became worn. Testers went into hyperdrive with comments like "simply a marvelous revelation that has genuinely elevated the status of motorcycling."

Honda CBX1000 (1978)

Engine type	Air-cooled DOHC, 24-valve transverse six
Displacement	1047cc
Bore x stroke	64.5 x 53.4 mm
Compression ratio	9.3:1
Carburetion	6 x 28 mm Keihins
Claimed power	105 BHP @ 9000 RPM
Transmission	5-speed
Electrics	12 V battery; 60/50 W headlamp
Frame	Tubular steel
Front suspension	Telescopic, no adjustment
Rear suspension	Twin shock absorbers, adjustable preload
Front brake	Twin 276 mm (10.9 in) discs
Rear brake	Single 295 mm (11.6 in) disc
Front tire	3.50 x 19 in
Rear tire	4.00 x 18 in
Wheelbase	1524 mm (60 in)
Seat height	813 mm (32 in)
Fuel capacity	20 liters (4.4 UK gal, 5.3 US gal)
Weight	260 kg (572 lb) wet

But unfortunately for Honda, the public was less impressed, particularly in America, where the bike did not go on sale until early 1979. The CBX was expensive compared to rivals' fours, without significantly increased performance. In America the slow-selling original Z model was followed a year later by the A version, which had air forks, reprofiled cams giving slightly less peak power, plus a new swingarm. (The CBX-B of 1981 was totally redesigned as a sport-tourer, with fairing, panniers, and Pro-Link monoshock, and gained some converts in the States.)

The CBX was a glorious attempt that failed, for rarely before or since can so much two-wheeled design genius have been deployed for so little reward. But at least, like some masterpiece by a long-dead artist, the Honda's impact is now belatedly acknowledged by members of the International CBX Owners' Association, which has branches in many countries worldwide. The CBX1000 was rejected in its day, but its place in motorcycling history is assured.

Below: Atmospheric brochure cover design did not succeed in making the expensive CBX a sales success, but the model's high-tech image gave Honda's credibility a boost. Opposite, left: The six was a pure high-performance machine that fully lived up to its Super Sport designation. Opposite, right: For such a big bike the Honda handled very well, and even had a generous amount of ground clearance. Opposite, below: Classy instrument console and low, clip-on handlebars added to the CBX's superior feel. The engine delivered smooth power from 2000rpm, before hitting warp drive at 6000rpm.

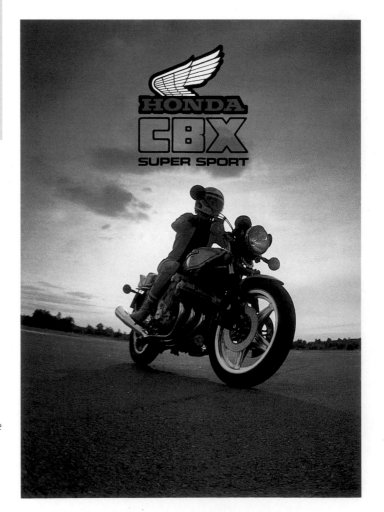

From *Cycle*, FEB. 1978

"The Six was not built for pragmatists. It was built for romantics, for people with soft spots in their hearts for mechanical maximum expressions, for people whose specific reasons for motorcycling match the CBX's specific reasons for being built.

Its European texture is a breakthrough for the Japanese motorcycle industry. Its engine performance is devastating, its high-speed handling and cornering clearance are remarkable, its drive-line character is unflawed and the linear responsiveness of every control and system is unique in all of motorcycling. It cannot be rationally compared to anything on the street, because nothing except a GP road racer is as narrowly committed to high-speed performance.

It embodies extravagance without vulgarity and high style without pretence—you see muscles and tendons, not chrome and fussiness. It has been designed, not decorated. There is no trashiness in the concept, and none in the execution. The CBX is an immensely flattering bike with perfect elegance and total class, and history will rank it with those rare and precious motorcycles which will never, ever be forgotten."

MV Agusta Magni 850

The sound starts as the tach needle hits 6500 RPM for the first time, and it's quite simply the loudest, most outrageous, and most utterly thrilling racket that I've ever experienced on a motorcycle.

Already, the sensation of riding this MV Agusta Magni has been heightened by its glorious noise. The moment the red-and-silver machine fires up, those four deliciously sculpted matte black Magni pipes emit a warbling, soulful bellow that raises the hairs on the back of your neck. When you pull away, the exhaust note rises in pitch and volume, drowning out the busy whir of the big motor's fast-spinning cam gears.

But it's when you wind open the throttle to its stop that the real magic happens. As the revs rise toward 7000 RPM and the bike surges forward harder, its exhaust note is suddenly transformed. The tuneful howl becomes a hard, aggressive, shatteringly loud and almost metallic *waaaaaaaaaaa* that threatens to split your eardrums.

It's a truly memorable (if thoroughly antisocial) experience, and along with the bike's speed it helps to explain why MV's "Gallarate Fire Engines" are still so revered, long after the racetrack dominance that brought the firm from north of Milan 17 consecutive 500cc world championships has become a distant memory.

Standard MV roadsters are rare and valuable, but most desirable of all are the small number which, like this one, have been uprated with a frame and chain-drive conversion by Arturo Magni. After MV's closure, the boss of the all-conquering grand prix team set up a tuning business nearby. This bike's 832cc engine features a Magni chain-drive conversion, and the frame is also a Magni original.

It is a stunning machine, gloriously evocative of the 500cc racebike on which Phil Read won MV's last world championship in 1974. Its shape and detailing is classically elegant: the champion's

No.1 digit in its old-style yellow plate on the fairing; the long and subtly curved tank leading back to a small and delicately shaped single seat; the holes drilled for lightness in foot controls and rear sprocket; the curve of the Magni pipes.

It was a treat just to sit on the bike, leaning forward to the narrow clip-ons and eyeballing the black-faced clocks, the simple pair of warning lights (just high beam and low oil pressure), the temperature gauge, and the damping adjusters at the top of the fork legs. When I pressed a button on the tinny-looking switchgear, the starter motor—tacked on below the motor, linked by twin belts and also acting as the generator—hauled the big four-cylinder lump into raucous life.

First gear went in smoothly with a flick up of the right boot, and I let out the fairly light clutch to pull away, immediately impressed by the smooth and tractable nature of the big, fire-breathing powerplant. Even so the MV was not really the bike for

dawdling round town, where its aggressive riding position and lack of steering lock made life uncomfortable.

Once on the open road it was a very different story. This Magni motor had been increased to 832cc in capacity by boring out the original 789cc MV 750S America unit. With a relatively high 10.3:1 compression ratio and some lightened engine parts, maximum power was up on the America's 75 BHP at 8500 RPM.

There was certainly enough power to make for strong acceleration, even before getting the Veglia tach's needle near the 9000 RPM red-line. Carburetion was crisp down to below 3000 RPM, and the MV gained speed with a smooth and steadily increasing force in the midrange. The five-speed gearbox was generally good, too, though the change from second to third required a firm boot.

At 6500 RPM the bike suddenly pulled harder, as it came on the cam with that ear-splitting sound that must have been audible

for miles around. No doubt the din made the bike seem even quicker than it was, but the flat-out Agusta certainly gave a mind-blowing impression of speed and excitement as it headed for a top whack of close to 140 mph (225 km/h).

Despite their expense and racetrack heritage, MV's roadster fours did not handle particularly well at high speed, partly due to the heavy shaft-drive apparatus. But Magni's chain conversion cured that problem. And the old maestro's frame, with its twin top tubes instead of the conventional MV single spine, gave some welcome extra rigidity.

This was still a pretty long and tall motorcycle, with old-fashioned steering geometry and a rather high center of gravity. But overall weight was a reasonable 200 kg (440 lb) compared to the 235 kg (517 lb) of a standard MV. And with a combination of Magni frame, hydraulic steering damper, and relatively modern suspension parts, this bike's handling was pretty good.

Low-speed steering was slow but neutral, and even in faster curves only the odd slight wobble got through to the bars. Suspension at both ends was very firm, particularly the rear Konis. On a couple of bumpy high-speed straights I ended up out of the seat, with my weight on the footpegs, while the bike bucked beneath me like a runaway horse.

Thankfully the twin front discs and four-piston Brembos gave plenty of stopping power, though the large rear disc locked at the hint of left-booted pressure. Grip from the modern 18-inch Metzelers far exceeded anything that an MV pilot would have enjoyed decades ago, too. It was a magical experience to come charging up to a bend, blip the quick-action throttle as I braked and hooked back a couple of gears, then force the bike into a bend and wind open the Dell'Ortos to go howling off again.

Every motorcyclist should have the chance, just once, to ride this most evocative of Seventies superbikes, and to dream of being a part of those glory days at Gallarate. The price of a Magni MV is high, very high, but it can take you to places that other bikes just can't reach.

MV Agusta Magni 850 (1978)

Engine type	Air-cooled DOHC, 8-valve transverse four
Displacement	832cc
Bore x stroke	68.8 x 56 mm
Compression ratio	10.3:1
Carburetion	4 x 27 mm Dell'Orto
Claimed power	80 BHP @ 8500 RPM
Transmission	Gear primary, 5-speed box, chain final
Electrics	12 V battery
Frame	Tubular steel twin cradle
Front suspension	38 mm Forcelle Italia telescopic, adjustable for compression and rebound damping
Rear suspension	Koni twin shock absorbers, adjustable for preload
Front brake	Twin 280 mm (11 in) discs
Rear brake	280 mm (11 in) disc
Front tire	110/80 x 18 in
Rear tire	150/70 x 18 in
Wheelbase	1400 mm (55.1 in)
Fuel capacity	19 liters (4.2 UK gal, 5 US gal)
Weight	200 kg (440 lb) dry

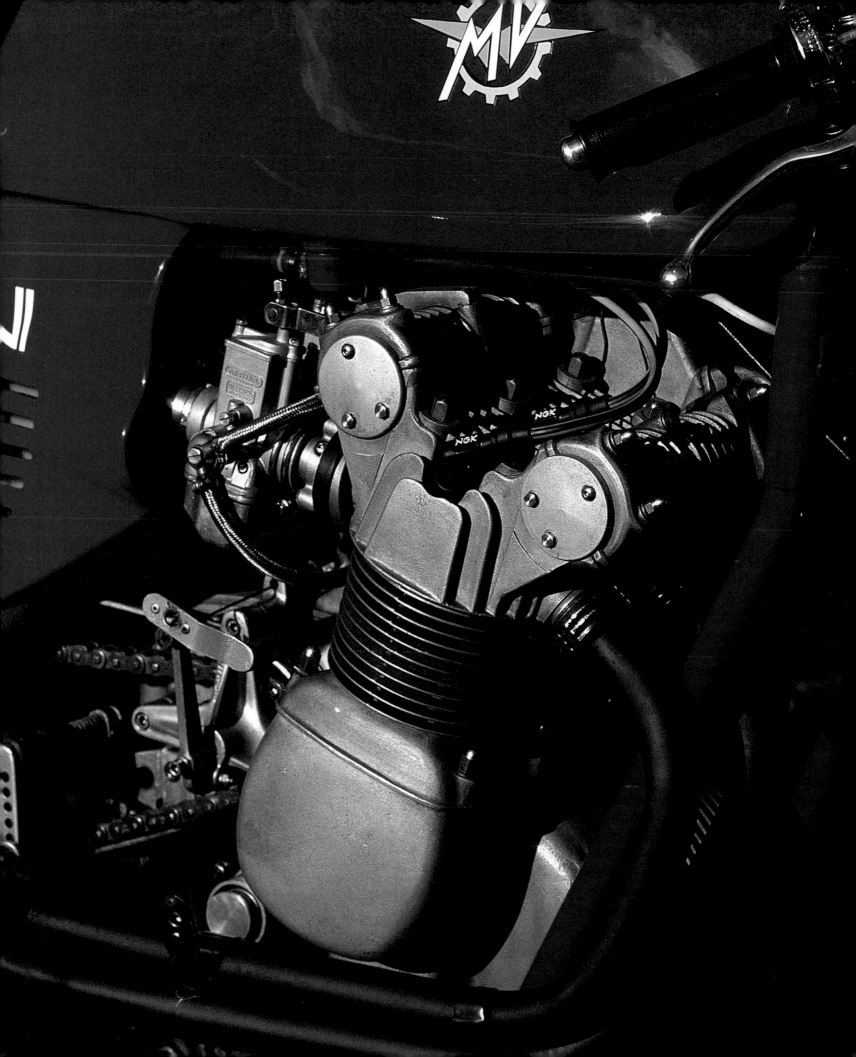

1978

Suzuki GS1000

It was a maneuver that any rider of a modern bike would make with barely a thought. When the traffic in the fast lane of the dual-carriageway cleared, I cracked open the throttle, accelerating hard up to about 100 mph (160 km/h) on a long, uphill straight. Then the road curved left so I braked slightly, flicked down a gear, and cranked into the turn, gradually feeding in the power to send the big Suzuki shooting smoothly off again.

Through the bend the bike behaved itself perfectly, soaking up the bumps and remaining under control at all times. Nothing special about that, these days. But the Suzuki in question was built in 1978—when it's doubtful whether any other Japanese bike of similar capacity could have taken the bend at the same speed without threatening to send me weaving or wobbling toward the edge of the road.

In its own quiet and unassuming way, the GS1000 was as much a landmark motorcycle as more celebrated early superbikes such as the CB750 and Z1. Its performance edge over contemporary machines—notably its direct rival the Z1000—was slight. But here, for the first time, was a big four whose chassis was a match for its motor.

For such an important machine, its basic format was very ordinary. Like the Z1000 and Suzuki's own recently released GS750, the GS Thou consisted of an air-cooled, eight-valve DOHC engine in a steel, duplex-cradle frame. Its forks held a 19-inch front wheel and there were twin rear shocks at the rear. Neat but understated styling was obviously derived from that of the GS750.

For all the similarities, the GS1000 had plenty of attractions of its own. Its frame was larger in places, and its tubular steel swingarm stronger. Its tires were wider, and it had an extra disc up front. Its forks were air-assisted, and its shocks could be adjusted through four rebound damping positions—giving the GS the most sophisticated suspension system yet seen on a mass-produced roadster.

The new engine was bigger and better, too. Dimensions of

Opposite: Suzuki's 997cc twin-cam engine was lighter and more powerful than the Kawasaki Z1000 unit on which it was so heavily based. Above: Pleasant but restrained styling echoed that of the smaller GS750- and 550-fours. Right: Sophisticated rear shocks were adjustable for rebound damping, and helped give the Suzuki excellent handling for a big four.

Right: The GS1000's round camshaft end caps distinguished this motor from Kawasaki's four, but its origins were clear. Suzuki's engineers had done their homework well, because the GS unit proved to be very reliable as well as immensely powerful. **Below right:** Air-assisted front forks allowed a degree of suspension tuning, and were stiff enough to maintain the bike's stability under hard braking. Typical Suzuki instrument panel included a revcounter, although the engine's midrange torque meant it was rarely necessary.

70 x 64.8cc gave a capacity of 997cc. Breathing through a bank of 26 mm Mikuni carbs, the Suzuki produced a claimed maximum of 87 BHP at 8000 RPM, four horses up on the Z1000. Concerted effort to reduce weight (including lighter flywheel, thinner cases, and no kick-starter) meant the GS1000 engine was slightly lighter than its smaller relation, let alone Kawasaki's bigger powerplant.

It all added up to the best four-cylinder motorcycle that Japan or anywhere else had yet produced. Straight-line performance was scorching, with a standing quarter-mile time of less than 12 seconds, and a top speed of over 135 mph (217 km/h). Midrange power delivery was just as impressive, and the Suzuki soon proved that it was extremely reliable as well.

Better still, the GS1000's chassis really was capable of keeping up. The bike was rock-steady at speed in a straight line, with no need for a steering damper. Even in bends that would have had

Suzuki GS1000 (1978)

Engine type	Air-cooled DOHC, 8-valve transverse four
Displacement	997cc
Bore x stroke	70 x 64.8 mm
Compression ratio	9.2:1
Carburetion	4 x 26 mm Mikunis
Claimed power	87 BHP @ 8000 RPM
Transmission	5-speed
Electrics	12 V battery; 60/55 W headlamp
Frame	Tubular steel cradle
Front suspension	Telescopic, air-assisted
Rear suspension	Twin shock absorbers, adjustable preload and rebound damping
Front brake	Twin 280 mm (11 in) discs
Rear brake	280 mm (11 in) disc
Front tire	3.50 x 19 in
Rear tire	4.50 x 17 in
Wheelbase	1537 mm (60.5 in)
Seat height	813 mm (32 in)
Fuel capacity	19 liters (4.2 UK gal, 5 US gal)
Weight	242 kg (533 lb) wet

most Japanese rivals wallowing in the wake of a hard-ridden Le Mans or 900SS, the Suzuki's frame rigidity and suspension control kept it in the game.

This unrestored 33,000 mile (53,000 km) GS had led a fairly pampered life. Its engine covers were slightly scratched, and there were a couple of small tears in its seat. But the red-and-white paintwork was sparkling, and the engine burst into life at the press of a button, with a typical mix of four-pot rustling and clutch rat-

Below: By modern standards the Suzuki, with its 19-inch front wheel and typical Seventies steering geometry, had heavy steering and required plenty of rider effort to corner quickly. Back in 1978, though, this was the best-handling open-class superbike yet from Japan. Sticky modern Dunlops mean this GS would be quicker through turns now than when it was new.

From *Motorcyclist*, MAR. 1978

"It gave me time to think. Here was a motorcycle much faster on the racetrack than me, one which could float to Florida and back with ease as well as zip around town with the agility of a 550. Honda builds the F2 for canyon racers, the K-model for local touring/commuting and the massive GL1000 for crossing continents. It only takes one Suzuki to do all this—primarily because of its adjustable suspension. And Herculean motor. And accurate seating position, although the seat itself is only average. Versatility through adjustability and solid design is the heart of the GS1000.

We'd need a long yellow pad to list the Suzuki's strong points. From the use of tapered-roller bearings in the steering head to its quiet paint job, the Suzuki is a well-conceived and well-executed motorcycle. Its back-to-basics approach gives the sporting rider an alternative to heavier bikes which might be faster but don't handle nearly as well. It also gives the touring rider a chance to be as sporty as he dares. If the best motorcycle truly is the simplest motorcycle, Suzuki gets the title hands down."

tle. Tickover was slightly too high and first gear went in with a loud clonk, but otherwise the GS was as well mannered as the day it left the showroom.

Ironically it was the bike's much-praised chassis that made the strongest initial impression—and not for the right reasons. At around 240 kg (530 lb) with its tank partly filled, the GS was reasonably light by 1978 standards. But the bike felt very heavy at slow speed, when its steering geometry and 19-inch front wheel meant I had to shove hard on the bars to tip it down into a bend.

The suspension hid its age better, and managed to combine a reasonably soft ride with good control over bumps. Air-assistance allowed the forks to be firmed up for fast riding or racing. Like the shocks, they worked well enough to make it clear why they were rated superior to most other production units in '78.

This bike's cast alloy wheels wore modern Dunlop rubber, which gave more grip than a GS rider would have had in the bike's heyday. Front brake feel at the handlebar was wooden, but the Suzuki could be stopped abruptly if given a hefty squeeze of the lever. (At least it could in the dry. Wet-weather braking was reportedly awful.)

The 87 BHP motor still felt mighty strong all these years later, especially in its willingness to pull from almost any revs. Just open

the throttle, and *go*. The five-speed gearbox was slick, and on the open road it was hardly needed. The Suzuki cruised happily at an indicated ton (160 km/h) with less than 6000 RPM on the clock, and stormed from 40 mph (64 km/h) to almost 140 mph (225 km/h) in top gear, if required.

This was phenomenal performance by 1978 standards, and especially impressive considering that the GS was Suzuki's first attempt at an open-class superbike. Apart from a few minor criticisms such as the lack of a pillion grab-rail, the GS's only real failing was perhaps that, for all its brilliance, it lacked charisma, even by Japanese standards.

This bike and the bikini-faired GS1000S that followed earned Suzuki a reputation for big four-strokes almost overnight. A great dynasty had been founded, but even so the GS1000 won't be remembered for that. More than anything, what makes this bike special is that after the release of the GS1000, that old phrase "Japanese bikes don't handle" never quite rang true again.

Kawasaki Z1-R

There was no doubt about which bike was king of the local roads when I was a bike-mad teenager back in 1978. I'd just graduated from a humble Honda trail bike to an old Triumph twin; my motorcycling mates had Japanese middleweights, mostly Suzuki and Yamaha two-strokes.

And one guy we'd see occasionally, though never get close enough to speak to, used to flash around the neighborhood on a brand new Z1-R. Some bike! To those of us brought up to regard Kawasaki's original Z1 as the definitive Japanese superbike, the silvery-blue café-racer factory special was one desirable piece of machinery.

This Z1-R and its rider certainly had quite a reputation in our biking circles. Unusually for those days, he rode in one-piece leathers—lime green and white ones, just like those worn by Kawasaki's road-race stars Mick Grant and Yvon Duhamel. But it was the bike that was the real star. As well as being the fastest bike in our local area, this was the most single-minded big-bore sportster that the Big K had yet produced.

Its powerplant was unchanged from that of the basic Z1000, which meant an air-cooled eight-valve, twin-cam four whose 70 x 66 mm dimensions gave a capacity of 1015cc. The standard bike's 26 mm Mikuni carbs were replaced by bigger 28 mm items, and the twin-pipe exhaust system was ditched for a four-into-one. Those mods raised max output by six horses to 90 BHP at 8000 RPM.

Kawasaki's awesome Seventies reputation had been forged by the power and strength of its engines, but the Z1000's chassis had come in for plenty of criticism over the years. Kawasaki didn't go to great lengths to improve matters, but they did add some gusseting under the headstock in an attempt to strengthen the twin-downtube steel frame.

Opposite: The Z1-R's paint scheme and angular styling were not to every Kawasaki fan's taste, but at least the bikini fairing gave some useful protection. Above: A four-into-one exhaust system meant the bike's left side view was strangely bare. Right: Firmer suspension added some cornering poise, despite the Kawasaki's considerable size and weight.

There were also uprated swingarm bearings for '78, in an attempt to cure the high-speed histrionics for which big Kawasakis had become known. Suspension was much modified, the forks gaining longer springs and revised damping, and the shocks being fitted with dual-rate springs. Wheels were cast alloy instead of wire-spoked, the front coming down an inch in size to 18 inches in diameter.

What did most to make the Z1-R special, though, was its bikini fairing and the angular styling theme that was carried throughout the bike, from the coffin-shaped tank and triangular side panels to the long, thin seat and the tailpiece. The fairing was made of fiberglass, and held an ammeter and fuel gauge, as well as the normal clocks and warning lights. Behind it were bolted handlebars whose slight raise was in contrast to the standard Z1000's high bars.

This unrestored, 23,000-mile (37,000 km) R fired up enthusiasti-

cally, its motor rustling and whirring in familiar fashion. Despite its aggressive look, this bike was not really a racy special. Its bars gave a slight lean forward, not an aggressive crouch, and footrests were fairly well forward. At 255 kg (560 lb) wet, the R was barely lighter than the stock Z1000, and its tall seat added to the feeling of size and weight.

My Z1-R riding hero had seemed rapid through the local lanes back in '78, but minor roads aren't this bike's natural habitat. It was here that the bike's size and crude suspension were most apparent. Kawasaki's attempt to improve handling had involved the traditional Italian method of firming up the forks and shocks, to the poin where the R rode like a plank at low speeds, passing on every bump through bars and seat.

Despite having slightly steeper geometry than the stock Z1000, the R took a lot of effort to haul around, too, thanks partly to its high center of gravity. At least this bike's modern Dunlop/Avon tire combination was a big improvement on the rubber of old. And the Z1-R's stoppers worked fairly well, too, hauling the bike up abruptly despite all that weight.

Predictably there was no need to worry about what the big four-cylinder engine was doing, because it was always ready to get to work at the merest twist of the throttle. Response at low revs was instant, and the midrange torque was strong enough to send the R forward *hard* from below 50 mph (80 km/h) in top. This elderly motor was impressively smooth, too, tingling slightly at around 5000 RPM and then clearing as it headed for the 8500 RPM red-line.

Kawasaki Z1-R (1978)

Engine type	Air-cooled DOHC, 8-valve transverse four
Displacement	1015cc
Bore x stroke	70 x 66 mm
Compression ratio	8.7:1
Carburetion	4 x 38 mm Mikunis
Claimed power	90 BHP @ 8000 RPM
Transmission	5-speed
Electrics	12 V battery; 60/55 W headlamp
Frame	Tubular steel cradle
Front suspension	Telescopic, no adjustment
Rear suspension	Twin shock absorbers, adjustable preload
Front brake	Twin 300 mm (11.8 in) discs
Rear brake	300 mm (11.8 in) disc
Front tire	3.50 x 18 in
Rear tire	4.00 x 18 in
Wheelbase	1506 mm (59.3 in)
Seat height	813 mm (32 in)
Fuel capacity	13 liters (2.9 UK gal, 3.4 US gal)
Weight	255 kg (560 lb) wet

Below: New shocks with dual-rate springs combined with uprated front forks and a braced frame to give better handling than that of the standard Z1000. High-speed stability was still less than perfect, though. Below right: Despite its imperfections, the Z1-R was hugely desirable to a generation of motorcyclists who had been captivated by the original Z1.

Straight-line performance was impressive, with a top speed of around 130 mph (210 km/h) and a quarter-mile time in the low 12-second bracket. Back in '78 that was serious speed. Only the GS1000 and CBX could do better, and then not by much. On a straight road the Kawa had an important edge, too, due to its small but efficient fairing.

On the other hand, it's likely that the bar-mounted fairing was partly to blame for the high-speed weave mentioned in some tests. General opinion was that the R's upgraded chassis simply delayed the onset of the Z1000's old handling failings. On crowded roads this bike didn't have much chance to misbehave, but it raced up to an indicated 110 mph (175 km/h) on the shortest of straights, and felt as though it would have held that speed forever.

Or at least until the fuel ran out, for another of the Z1-R's weaknesses was its tiny tank, which allowed less than 100 miles (160 km) of hard riding. The inaccurate fuel gauge wasn't much help, either. In contrast the R's self-canceling indicators were a sophisticated touch, and its halogen headlamp was a revelation in '78.

From *SuperBike*, MAY 1978

"One moment the bike is behaving itself with panache and style, and you start to think that here is a new breed of Japanese motorcycle, one that actually handles, but then the depressing reality returns. Overworked suspension at the rear gives out with a gasp of exhaustion, and there you are, as if plunged into a time warp, wrestling with a bike that is just plain old oriental in habits and character, bucking like a bronco.

The four cylinders with the DOHC produce the stunning power that The Big Zee is famous for. Not only does it launch the bike into near-orbit; around town the big four purrs as sweetly as a 500, providing tractable power with no strings attached.

Better late than never, Kawasaki. Keep it up and one day the usurpers to your throne will be taught that to overthrow a king you have to kill him absolutely stone dead, not just relegate him to third place."

All in all there were rather too few neat touches to the Z1-R, and too many areas where Kawasaki had allowed the opposition to leap ahead. Despite its new clothes, upgraded engine, and improved chassis, the Z1-R was not a dramatic improvement over the ordinary Z1000. But it was still the best big Kawasaki yet, and for plenty of riders, that was more than enough.

1978

Yamaha XS1100

My first ride on an XS1100 was many years ago, but the memory still brings me out in a cold sweat. Dunlop had assembled a varied selection of machinery for a big tire launch in southern Ireland, and I'd ended up on the XS. The roads were twisty and bumpy, the pace was hot, and the Yamaha was truly horrible as it lurched and wobbled its way around in the company of a gang of lighter and much better-handling superbikes.

At the time of that launch the XS1100 was already a few years old, and those bumpy roads emphasized handling flaws that had not been cured since its release in 1978. Yamaha's problem was that there was little that they could do—short of a complete redesign— about the high-speed behavior of the XS1100, whose nickname the "Excess Eleven" was well and truly deserved. The XS was simply too big, heavy, and powerful for its chassis.

All of which makes it rather surprising that, all these years later, I had a great time riding this big, bluey-black bruiser of a motorbike. On a bright, blustery day, it was good fun to potter down some winding lanes on the Yam, enjoying its effortless

power delivery, smoothness, and comfort—and with the intervening years having removed much of the temptation to push too hard in the bends.

The XS1100 itself can't have improved in the meantime, so my change of heart can only be due to my approaching the bike with radically different expectations. Anticipation had been high in 1978, when the Eleven had been introduced hot on the heels of the XS750 triple. But Yamaha's flagship had the misfortune to arrive in a vintage year that saw Suzuki's GS1000, in particular, raise the yardstick for superbike chassis performance.

There was never much wrong with the XS's mighty air-cooled, four-cylinder engine, even so. The twin-cam, eight-valve unit

Opposite: With the sun shining, the fuel tank full, and a straight road stretching out ahead, the broad saddle of the XS1100 was a very pleasant place to be. Above: Styling did little to disguise the Yamaha's considerable size. Right: Rear shocks struggled to cope with the XS's weight and shaft final drive. Stubby exhaust mufflers, like the high bars, denote US market model.

Yamaha XS1100 (1978)

Engine type	Air-cooled DOHC, 8-valve transverse four
Displacement	1101cc
Bore x stroke	71.5 x 68.6 mm
Compression ratio	9.2:1
Carburetion	4 x 34 mm Mikunis
Claimed power	95 BHP @ 8000 RPM
Transmission	5-speed
Electrics	12 V battery; 60/55 W headlamp
Frame	Tubular steel cradle
Front suspension	Telescopic, adjustable preload
Rear suspension	Twin shock absorbers, adjustable preload
Front brake	Twin 298 mm (11.7 in) discs
Rear brake	Single 298 mm (11.7 in) disc
Front tire	3.50 x 19 in
Rear tire	4.50 x 17 in
Wheelbase	1575 mm (62 in)
Seat height	800 mm (31.5 in)
Fuel capacity	18 liters (4 UK gal, 4.7 US gal)
Weight	273 kg (601 lb) wet

Opposite, from left: Twin-disc front brakes were impressively powerful, though hard use tended to overwhelm the relatively weedy front forks. Yamaha's 1101cc four was softly tuned and hugely flexible, yet still produced an impressive peak output of 95 BHP. Its drive shaft was reasonably unobtrusive, but the five-speed gearbox was a weakness. The angular shape of the headlamp was echoed in the instrument panel, which included a fuel gauge. High handlebars encouraged a fairly gentle riding style, as did the Yamaha's ponderous high-speed handling.

featured shaft final drive, like the XS750. Its extra cylinder brought capacity up to 1101cc, and raised peak power output to a claimed 95 BHP at 8000 RPM.

The Yamaha's chassis was based around a steel twin-cradle frame that was extensively braced and very heavy. It held a swingarm that combined box-section steel on one side and the drive-shaft housing on the other. Braking was by a triple-disc setup, with front and rear rotors of identical 298 mm (11.7 in) diameter in period fashion.

Less conventional was the Yamaha's styling, which combined a bulbous fuel tank and side panels with a rectangular headlamp and square instruments. To most eyes the XS was plain ugly, its shape doing nothing at all to hide the bike's 273 kg (600 lb) of fuelled-up weight.

This American-spec XS, differing from the European model mainly in its higher handlebars, smaller tank, and shorter silencers, had a little over 10,000 miles (16,000 km) on the clock and was very clean, its paintwork almost immaculate and its alloy and chrome gleaming. The XS is a tall bike with a wide seat, and you're aware of its size and weight the moment you haul it up off the sidestand. But this bike's pull-back bars gave a pleasantly

relaxed riding position, and the motor whirred into life instantly at a press of the button.

Winding open the four 34 mm Mikuni carbs anywhere between 2000 RPM and 7000 RPM sent smooth torque gushing out, as the Yamaha headed for its top speed of a little over 130 mph (210 km/h). There was barely the hint of a power step, and little to be gained from thrashing the big motor to its 8500 RPM red-line.

Despite criticism of the transmission in contemporary road tests, I found this bike's five-speed box fine, and the shaft drive reasonably free of slack. The gearbox is just about the only weakness of the generally very strong motor, though, as even low-mileage XS1100s have been known to jump out of second gear.

Handling was marginal even when the bike was brand new, although thankfully the XS didn't turn out to be quite the wobble-prone monster I remembered. The big four felt ponderous at slow speed, but its suspension did a fair job of soaking up bumps, and straight-line stability was pretty good. Even so, the big XS did not encourage aggressive cornering of the type that I'd been trying to make it perform all those years ago.

If I took a medium-speed bend at seven-tenths speed, it whirred round happily. When I upped the pace to eight-tenths, the steering started to feel vague, while the rear end began to pogo gently as the bike's weight and drive shaft got the better of its shocks. By nine-tenths the Yam was flapping its bars and lurching about like a dinghy in a hurricane—but I'm talking from vividly preserved memory here because I felt no desire to prove that all over again.

Hard braking in anything other than a straight line was guaranteed to send the big Yam gyrating around its spindly forks, too, but at least the triple-disc setup gave a reasonable amount of stopping power. The Yamaha was also a practical bike. Its seat was comfortable, with a grab-rail for the pillion, and there was the 1978 novelty of a fuel gauge alongside the electronic tachometer.

Back in the late Seventies, such attractions were not enough to

make the XS1100 competitive against lighter and better-handling opposition, while the American touring riders who would have appreciated its smoothness and comfort generally turned to Honda's Gold Wing. Yamaha added an innovative two-piece fairing that turned the XS into a more comfortable but also even more cumbersome tourer. Neither that bike nor the black, bikini-faired XS1100 Sport really caught on, though the latter gained something of a cult following.

The Yamaha's lack of reputation gives it one advantage these days, though, in that a clean XS such as this one costs less than its more successful contemporary rivals—whose performance advantage, so crucial then, is far less important now. Two decades and more after its launch, maybe the XS1100's time has finally come.

From *SuperBike*, APR. 1978

"When this behemoth of a motorcycle actually hits a corner at anything approaching interesting speeds then it takes a good deal of muscle to lay it down. While the Yamaha doesn't disgrace itself in corners (not as much as some Z1000s I have known, for example) it doesn't commend itself either.

It's also a big, powerful tourer, and well-nigh impossible to stretch to anywhere near any kind of limit on the straight. The massive engine wasn't under any strain at any time. The rider meets the limitations of the road long before any kind of performance horizon comes into sight. Power floods in effortlessly all the way across the wide, meaty powerband.

Supremely comfortable, the 1100 is the highway cruiser par excellence. From the moment one steps on board the impression is of bullet proof muscle. This is reinforced by the sheer sound of the engine."

Laverda Jota

It had been a long day on the road, and the owner of the big Laverda triple was keen to get home. By now darkness had fallen, the temperature had dropped, and he still had some distance to cover. Leaning forward against the breeze, he wound the throttle back and saw the speedometer needle rise toward 100 mph (160 km/h) as the three-cylinder motor breathed more deeply.

For several minutes he held the Laverda at a steady speed, pleased at how smooth its motor felt for a 180-degree crankshaft triple that was only just run-in. He didn't worry when he saw the blue flashing lights of a police car up ahead; merely rolled off the throttle and eased down below 70 mph (115 km/h). But then he glanced over his shoulder—to see a string of police vehicles, their lights flashing, sirens wailing, and engines racing in a desperate attempt to catch up with him.

Even more than two decades after its launch, a late-Seventies Laverda triple is still fast enough to get you into serious trouble with the law. (The unfortunate rider was banned from driving after that incident on the way home from bringing me the bike to test.)

But most of the time, that high performance was the greatest asset of the triples from Breganze in northeastern Italy.

The 981cc Jota and its big brother the 1116cc Mirage were among the fastest, toughest, and most charismatic of Seventies superbikes. Both models were essentially tuned-up versions of the Breganze factory's standard three-cylinder superbikes. British Laverda importer Slater Brothers created the Jota first, by uprating the standard 3CL triple with high-compression pistons, endurance

Opposite: The big and brutal Jota might not have handled with the finesse of some Italian rivals, but it was as exciting to ride in corners as it was in a straight line. Above: Styling was simple, effective, and dominated by the big three-cylinder engine. Right: The Jota's 981cc motor was a tuned version of the Italian marque's standard dohc unit.

Right: Laverda's most glamorous late-Seventies stablemates were the Jota and its 1116cc derivative, the Mirage. The latter, which like the Jota was created by UK importer Slater Brothers, was essentially the Italian factory's unimaginatively named 1200 model, tuned with the Jota's hot cams and loud exhaust. Laverda also used the Mirage name in some markets for triples without the tuning parts.

race cams, and a loud pipe. That lifted power output to 90 BHP and produced a mighty machine that was a match for anything on the road or production racetrack. Before long the Jota was available in other markets, too.

In 1978, when Laverda bored out the DOHC three-cylinder engine to 1116cc and fitted flat handlebars and a larger dual-seat to produce the softer, more practical 1200, the Slaters struck again. With no production racing plans this time, they left the compression ratio at the standard 8:1 but added the endurance race camshafts and the Jota exhaust system, increasing performance considerably. The Mirage was born.

The saddle of a hot Laverda triple is still a magical place to be. In the smaller model's case, you lean forward across the long tank to the low, adjustable "Jota bars," that big air-cooled engine whirring away below. Japanese switchgear and clocks hint that Laverdas were in many ways the most sophisticated of Italian superbikes.

Passing time may have seen the Jota's performance outclassed, but I didn't have to ride far to be reminded that the triple can still get the adrenalin flowing. This is a bike capable of well over two miles (3.2 km) per minute, after all, and the noise and vibration with which it accelerated only added to the spine-tingling sensation of speed.

In fact the Jota was slightly smoother and more civilized than normal, because it had been fitted with lower-compression 3CL pistons (9:1 from 10:1) and an improved ignition system during a top-to-toe restoration. It pulled cleanly and hard through the midrange, could even be trickled along with as little as 2000 RPM showing on the tach, and was very easy to ride, helped by an efficient right-foot, five-speed gearbox.

And the Jota sure stormed forward with plenty of enthusiasm when I wound open the trio of 32 mm Dell'Orto carbs. As the revs rose the 180-degree motor made itself felt more through

the bars, seat, and pegs. But I was enjoying myself far too much to care as the Jota howled toward a top speed of about 140 mph (225 km/h).

The Jota didn't handle quite as well as its rivals in that magnificent Italian triumvirate of the mid-Seventies, Ducati's 900SS and Moto Guzzi's Le Mans Mk1, partly because it was the heaviest of the three, as well as the most powerful. But for road use the triple was fine, and more than a match for its Japanese opposition.

This bike had the benefit of rebuilt forks and new Koni shocks, and stayed impressively stable. With over 230 kg (506 lb) of weight and old-fashioned steering geometry, quick direction changes needed a fair bit of pressure on those low and fairly narrow bars. But the triple's steering was very neutral and its suspension coped with all but the biggest bumps without jarring.

The Laverda's Michelin Macadams gave plenty of grip, too,

despite being so narrow by modern standards (the rear a mere 120/90 x 18 in). Ground clearance was fine for road use, and the only chassis part that showed its age was the Brembo front brake. When new, the twin-disc stopper was state of the art, but the lever needed a very firm squeeze to make the Jota slow with real urgency.

That was the only real criticism, though, of a bike that was seriously enjoyable, and whose performance has kept it highly desirable, even after all these years. A Laverda Jota is no longer the fastest thing on two wheels, but as well as a two-wheeled legend, it remains a supremely exhilarating machine.

Laverda Jota 1000 (1979)

Engine type	Air-cooled DOHC, 6-valve triple
Displacement	981cc
Bore x stroke	75 x 74 mm
Compression ratio	10:1 (bike tested 9:1)
Carburetion	Three 32 mm Dell'Ortos
Claimed power	90 BHP @ 8000 RPM
Transmission	5-speed
Electrics	12 V battery
Frame	Tubular steel cradle
Front suspension	38 mm telescopic Marzocchi
Rear suspension	Two Koni dampers, adjustments for preload and rebound damping
Front brake	Twin 280 mm (11 in) discs
Rear brake	Single 280 mm (11 in) disc
Front tire	100/90 x 18 in
Rear tire	120/90 x 18 in
Wheelbase	1460 mm (57.5 in)
Seat height	813 mm (32 in)
Fuel capacity	20 liters (4.4 UK gal, 5.3 US gal)
Weight	237 kg (521 lb) wet

From *Cycle World*, Nov. 1977

"It's as elemental as a rock slide and as direct as the charge of a rhinoceros. In a world of rip-snorting two-wheeled quarter horses, here is this great, gaunt brute dredged up from somewhere in the Pleistocene.

You throw a leg over this brute only when you want to test your personal limits. The limits of the bike itself are beyond, say, 90 to 95 percent of us. The faster it goes, the better it gets, and you're probably going to run out of road or nerve or skill or all three before you're scraping anything.

No matter what they do to you out there in the day-to-day jungle, you know at the end of the day you can wrap yourself around the Jota and fly away into another realm. Who can put a price on that kind of therapy?"

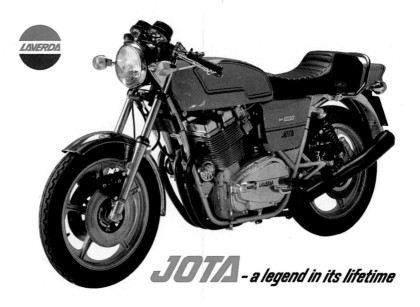

LAVERDA

JOTA - *a legend in its lifetime*

Left: Jotas were fitted with cast wheels and Brembo disc brakes, unlike Laverda's first triple the 3C, which had been launched in 1973 with wire wheels and drums. Above: The Jota legend was forged by a 140mph (225km/h) top speed that made it unofficially the world's fastest streetbike, and, in Britain, by Laverda rider Pete Davies' victories in the national production racing championship.

Kawasaki Z1300

When you ride the Big Six now, it's hard to imagine what all the fuss was about. Loping lazily along a narrow road with its big engine spinning smoothly, its twin silencers burbling, its suspension soaking up the bumps, and its raised handlebars, broad seat and forward-set footpegs adding to the comfortable ride, the Kawasaki seems docile and inoffensive.

Even when you crack open the throttle to send the bike whistling rapidly toward its top speed of almost 140 mph (225 km/h), the sensation is one of smoothness and refinement, as much as of power and speed.

But things were very different in 1979, when the Z1300 was unleashed on a motorcycling public that had not seen its like before. The Kawasaki's monstrous, 1286cc engine added water-cooling, shaft drive, and numerous complex technical features to the transverse six-cylinder DOHC layout that Honda had pioneered a year earlier with the CBX1000.

This was more than simply motorcycling's mightiest mass-produced powerplant. Its peak output of 120 BHP at 8000 RPM

was 15 BHP higher than that of the CBX, and gave a significant 25 BHP advantage over the best fours. Weighing over 300 kg (660 lb) with fuel, the Z1300 was considerably heavier than any other unfaired bike. And its brutal, angular styling seemed designed to emphasize, rather than disguise, its enormous size.

With the world in the midst of an oil crisis and public sentiment turning toward efficiency and economy, the Z1300's untimely arrival—coinciding with the West German government's introduction of a 100 BHP limit—caused a sensation. Road testers of the day used words like "outrageous" and "overkill." Some even predicted that the Kawasaki would lead to motorcycles being banned altogether.

If ever a motorcycle was designed around an engine, it's this

Opposite: The liquid-cooled Kawasaki's radiator reduced its six-cylinder engine's visual impact from the front, but this was unmistakably one very substantial motorbike. Above: Kawasaki enlarged parts, including the fuel tank and frame, in an attempt to make the Z1300 look normal. Right: Slab-sided styling theme extended to the informative instrument console.

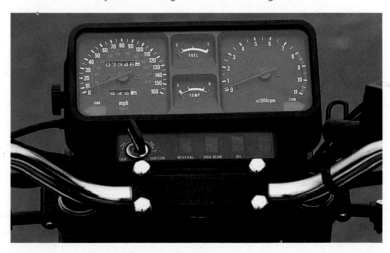

Kawasaki Z1300 (1979)

Engine type	Water-cooled DOHC, 12-valve transverse six
Displacement	1286cc
Bore x stroke	62 x 71 mm
Compression ratio	9.9:1
Carburetion	3 x 32 mm twin-choke Mikunis
Claimed power	120 BHP @ 8000 RPM
Transmission	5-speed
Electrics	12V battery; 60/55 W headlamp
Frame	Tubular steel cradle
Front suspension	41 mm telescopic, air assisted
Rear suspension	Twin shock absorbers, adjustable preload
Front brake	Twin 260 mm (10.2 in) discs
Rear brake	250 mm (9.8 in) disc
Front tire	4.30 x 18 in
Rear tire	5.10 x 17 in
Wheelbase	1587 mm (62.5 in)
Seat height	813 mm (32 in)
Fuel capacity	27 liters (5.9 UK gal, 7.1 US gal)
Weight	305 kg (670 lb) wet

Below: The shaft final drive system added yet more weight, but the rear shocks did an admirable job of keeping it under control. Opposite, left: Kawasaki's monstrous 1286cc, dohc six produced 120 BHP and was by some distance the most powerful production bike of the Seventies. Although indisputably huge, heavy, and thirsty, it was also impressively smooth, tractable, and reliable. Opposite, right: Handling was improbably good for such a gigantic machine, and the Z1300 even had a reasonable amount of ground clearance.

one. At almost 130 kg (286 lb) without its drive shaft, the engine on its own weighed more than most 125cc bikes. Water-cooling allowed the cylinders to be spaced closely together. Long-stroke dimensions helped keep Kawasaki's six slightly narrower than Honda's, despite running its alternator on the end of the crankshaft.

Carburetion was by a trio of twin-choke Mikunis, in contrast to the CBX's broader bank of six. If some of the Kawasaki's visual impact was reduced by the simple twin-silencer exhaust system, and from the front by the radiator, the row of gleaming down-pipes and the smooth engine cases ensured the Z13 still looked impressive.

Like much of the engine, the chassis was conventional in all but size. The twin cradle frame's steel tubes were thicker than normal, and held leading-axle forks that, at 41 mm in diameter, were equally sturdy. Only from close up was it clear that parts such as the tank, seat, and bodywork were also larger than normal.

The Z1300's angular lines extended to the clock console, head-light, indicators, and even the ignition key. It was as though the designers were boasting that with this much power there was no need to worry about streamlining. And to a certain extent, there

wasn't. When I hit the button the engine came to life with eerie smoothness, barely a rustle from the engine, and a low exhaust note that hinted at the power within.

Straight-line performance was undeniably impressive. The Z1300 ripped through the standing quarter in under 12 seconds, leaving behind a high-pitched howl and a trail of rear-tire rubber as it blasted away from the line. There was plenty of acceleration at lower engine speeds, too, which allowed rapid progress without much use of the five-speed gearbox.

With no fewer than four flexible couplings in the drive train, the transmission felt very smooth. In top gear the thirteen pulled clean-ly from just over 2000 RPM. From there the motor simply got stronger and stronger, with no real power step and with an unburstable feel that was borne out by impressive reliability.

Even the most critical of late-Seventies testers had to admit that Kawasaki had done a good job with the thirteen's handling. The combination of beefy frame and competent suspension made the bike much less of a handful than it could have been, even at speed. At town pace the Z1300's long wheelbase helped make for easy maneuvering, despite the weight.

The air-assisted forks were rigid and well damped, and the shocks coped well despite the heavy shaft-drive rear end. Although the big bike's ability to change direction quickly brought to mind one of the Kawasaki group's container ships, it felt reassuringly neutral and stable once into a curve. There was even enough

ground clearance for an enthusiastic lean angle before the stands and footrests touched down.

Its triple-disc braking setup was much praised in 1979 but, although the combination of 260 mm (10.2 in) front discs and twin-piston calipers gave reasonable power, the lever was spongy. All that weight really became noticeable when I had to slow down in a hurry, too, despite the grip of this bike's modern Metzelers.

If the Z1300 had a weakness in 1979, though, it was simply that for all its horsepower and technology, it didn't do anything that rival fours couldn't manage much more cheaply. The six may have been slightly faster and smoother than the fours in a straight line, but its weight and windswept riding position made that of little practical value.

Inevitably the Z1300 was expensive, as well as heavy on tires and fuel, its thirst proving particularly unfortunate given the oil crisis raging at the time of its launch. Relatively few riders were prepared to pay the extra, and the Japanese firms realized that their fixation with size and power had gone too far.

Even so, the six made up for lack of instant sales success with remarkable longevity that saw it still in production, almost unchanged, nine years after its launch. If the giant bike's performance ultimately failed to match its technology, it was still a bold and exciting machine. And as the final explosion in the Seventies' horsepower war, the Z1300 made an impact that matched its amazing size.

From *SuperBike*, OCT. 1979

"Will there ever be another motorcycle like the Z1300? Will another manufacturer ever have the audacity to let such an outrageous machine escape from the drawing board onto the streets? Will ordinary bikers ever again have the chance of discovering at first hand what if feels like to have 120 horses champing at the bit?

I doubt it. Given the current oil-starved state of the world it's a fair bet that to the big K goes the honor of having the final word on the subject of hyperbiking.

As an exercise in corporate one-upmanship it's a dazzling success, which isn't altogether surprising considering that this is its true *raison d'être*. What *is* surprising is that lurking under the tinsel and technology, and almost secondary to this central purpose, is a surprisingly good heavyweight touring bike.

Comparisons? The 1300's unique, it's in a class of its own and will probably remain so for ever."

Epilogue

Rarely can a decade be defined as precisely as the Seventies was by its first and last significant superbikes. Just as the original Honda CB750 began the modern motorcycling era with its unprecedented sophistication, so the Kawasaki Z1300 of ten years later was the perfect final statement.

Until the mighty six, Japanese superbikes in particular had been getting bigger and more complex with every passing year. But the manufacturers changed direction in the Eighties. With some notable exceptions (such as the turbo bikes produced by all four Japanese firms), the machines that followed were less extravagant—evolutionary rather than revolutionary. They were more powerful and refined than those that had gone before, certainly, but most were developed from models that had begun life in the previous decade.

The Japanese inline four became firmly established as the dominant design (although Honda put much effort into a V4 family that still lives on). Development certainly did not cease. Suzuki's stylish Katana 1100, Yamaha's capable FJ1100, and Kawasaki's sleek and sophisticated GPz900R moved the game forward in a variety of different directions. The motorcycle world enthusiastically welcomed developments, including fairings, liquid-cooled engines, and single-shock rear suspension.

By the middle of the Eighties the old air-cooled, twin-shock superbikes were history, and the face of the future had arrived in the fully faired shape of Suzuki's ultra-light GSX-R750 race-replica. Many revisions later, the GSX-R is still a current model, its four-cylinder lineage traceable back past that first 1985 machine all the way to 1977 and the GS750, Suzuki's first big four-stroke.

And Suzuki is far from alone in having that continuity, for the influence of the Seventies superbike class can be seen in most manufacturers' line-ups. Ducati's latest sportsters are V-twins, just like the old 750 Sport and 900SS. Modern Moto Guzzis and Harley-Davidsons still point their twin cylinders in distinctively differing directions. After a long break, Triumph is back with a range of new triples. And the latest inline fours from Honda, Kawasaki, and Yamaha all have their roots in the Seventies—the decade that shaped modern motorcycling.